Faith First

Legacy Edition

At Home
Family Guide

Author
Mary Beth Jambor

Catechetical Advisor
Jacquie Jambor

RESOURCES FOR CHRISTIAN LIVING®

www.FaithFirst.com

Faith First Legacy Edition At Home Family Guide

Advisors and Consultants

Rev. Louis J. Cameli, S.T.D.
Rev. Robert Duggan, S.T.D.
Elaine McCarron, SCN, M.Div.
Rev. Frank McNulty, S.T.D.
Rev. Ronald J. Nuzzi, Ph.D.

General Editor • Ed DeStefano
Production Manager • Jenna Nelson
Senior Production Editor • Laura Fremder
Art and Design Director • Lisa Brent
Photo Research • Susan Smith
Senior Designer • Pat Bracken
Senior Editor • Patricia A. Classick
Cover Design • Kristy Howard

President • Maryann Nead

Acknowledgments and Credits appear on page 128.

NIHIL OBSTAT
Rev. Robert Coerver
Censor Librorum

IMPRIMATUR
† Most Rev. Charles V. Grahmann
Bishop of Dallas

October 1, 2004

The Nihil Obstat and Imprimatur are official declarations that the material reviewed is free from doctrinal or moral error. No implication is contained therein that those granting the Nihil Obstat and Imprimatur agree with the contents, opinions, or statements expressed.

Send all inquiries to:
RCL • Resources for Christian Living
200 East Bethany Drive
Allen, TX 75002-3804

Toll Free 877-275-4725
Fax 800-688-8356

Visit us at www.FaithFirst.com

Printed in the United States of America
Color Dynamics, Inc. Allen, Texas

20509   ISBN 0-7829-1085-8

1 2 3 4 5 6 7 8 9 10
05 06 07 08 09 10 11

Contents

Welcome to Faith First®

As the creators of the **Faith First Legacy Edition**© program we believe:

- Faith is both a gift from God and our free response to God.

- Faith includes not only an intellectual understanding of doctrine but also a conversion of heart and the adoption of a way of life.

- Faith grows and develops throughout all of life.

- Faith is to be lived and is best lived in community.

- Being a person of faith means looking at our actions and the world in a way different from the way people who are not people of faith do.

- All of life changes when we see things and people through eyes of faith.

Faith First is based on that vision of faith.

Faith First Legacy Edition At Home Family Guide helps you help your children understand both what we believe as Catholics and also how to live out those beliefs. This is the process that Jesus used to teach his disciples. When the disciples lived the teachings of Jesus, they discovered the difference that faith made in their lives and in the lives of others.

Faith First Legacy Edition At Home Family Guide helps you use this simple process used by Jesus. It is the teaching process that is repeated throughout the **Faith First** program. Discovering the difference faith makes in our lives is at the heart of **Faith First.**

Content

Faith First provides you and your children with a balanced presentation of doctrine, Scripture, and the Church's liturgical seasons. These themes are essential elements in a person's faith formation. Written in age-appropriate language and enhanced with compelling photos and illustrations, **Faith First** helps Catholic children recognize that what we believe, how we worship, how we live, and how we pray make a difference in our lives.

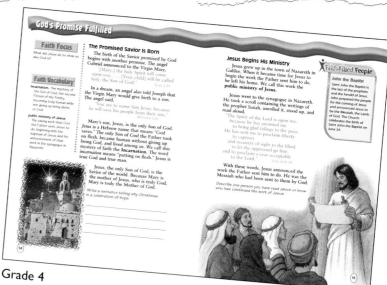

Grade 4

Grade 3

Doctrine. The doctrine chapters in **Faith First** are based on the four parts of the *Catechism of the Catholic Church*, namely, Creed, Worship and Sacraments, Morality, and Prayer.

Scripture. Each grade level of **Faith First** has special core Scripture chapters. Each Scripture chapter has three distinctive elements, namely, "Bible Background," "Reading the Word of God," and "Understanding the Word of God."

Liturgical Seasons. The twenty-three **Faith First** seasonal lessons provide you and your children with the opportunity to prayerfully participate in the liturgical year.

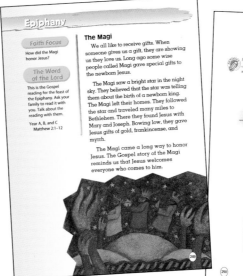

Grade 2

Features

We would like to share with you a few of the important features of the **Faith First Legacy Edition** student book.

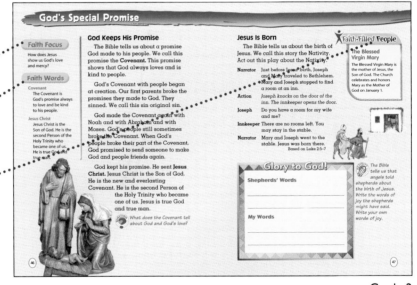

Grade 3

Unit Opener.
Assesses the children's prior knowledge about the key faith concepts presented in the unit as well as their expectations.

Chapter Opener.
Features a photograph or illustration that visually captures the faith focus of the chapter.

Grade 3

Each chapter of **Faith First Legacy Edition** has three consistent features.

Faith Focus.
Prepares your children for learning the content.

Faith Words.
Defines faith concepts.

Faith-Filled People.
Introduces saints and others who have lived exemplary lives and serve as models for young Catholics.

Grade 2

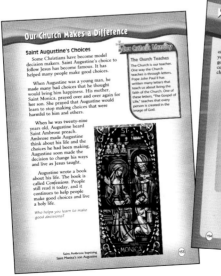

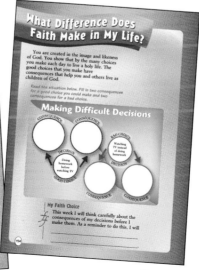

What Difference Does Faith Make?
These pages reveal the heart of the **Faith First** program. Each week the children are invited to make a practical and concrete faith decision to put into practice what they have learned.

Grade 4

How does faith happen in families first?

Long before your children were old enough for school or any formal religion program, they were already beginning to grow in faith. They had already been living and growing in the midst of a community of faith—their family.

What does it say to your children that one of the most important occasions of their lives was the day of their Baptism? Even though they have no conscious recollection of that day, they have seen photographs, they have heard the stories, and they know their godparents. When these family stories are told and retold, your children recognize the importance of those events, and they begin to gather impressions about faith and about religion.

What does it say to children that your family prays at mealtime? At bedtime? While you may not think of this as "teaching," your children are learning much about faith lived in the care of God who loves them and hears their prayers. And when a loved one is ill and your family prays for recovery, your children learn that God is with us even in the most sad and frightening moments of life.

From earliest experiences children come to know God through creation. Gradually, even the youngest child is introduced to the stories of Jesus. This is the beginning of readiness to hear and embrace the Gospel.

As your children attended Mass throughout early childhood, they came to know that there was something special about the place where they gathered with you and other members of the parish. Even as little children they recognized that special actions and events happened there. Soon they wanted to participate in Holy Communion.

Faith-filled moments permeate all of family life. It is true: faith happens in families first. And you as parents are blessed with the love and grace to foster your children's spiritual growth. Indeed, as parents you are uniquely able to teach your children—first because you yourselves are persons of faith and second because you are parents.

What does the Church ask of us as parents?

In his 1994 *Letter to Families,* Pope John Paul II reached out to families. He writes: *"Parents are the first and most important educators* of their own children, and they also possess a *fundamental competence* in this area: they are *educators because they are parents."* (16)

The letter continues: "What I offer, then, is *an invitation:* an invitation addressed especially to you, dearly beloved husbands and wives, fathers and mothers, sons and daughters. It is an invitation to all the particular Churches to remain united in the teaching of the apostolic truth." (23)

What is our parental role in religious education?

The Church views the role of parents in the religious formation of children as both a privilege and an obligation. When they present their children to the Church to be baptized, Catholic parents clearly are distinctly reminded that they have the responsibility "of training them in the practice of the faith" (Rite of Baptism of Children).

This vision of the role of parents in the religious formation of their children was explained in more detail in the *General Directory for Catechesis.* The English translation of this important document of the Church, which presents the principles and vision of catechesis, was published in 1998. In it the Church explicitly speaks of parents as the primary educators of their children.

The document emphasizes the tenderness and respect that parents bring to this vocation of training children in the practice of the faith. It is through the living witness of parents that children first experience the faith. This experience is irreplaceable and lasts throughout life. It is this religious formation that is the foundation of all other forms of religious education a person receives. This responsibility of parents is a true ministry. Through Matrimony parents receive the ministry and the grace to share their faith with their children so that their family life is a true journey of faith for them and their children (see *General Directory for Catechesis* 226–227).

Each theme of **Faith First Legacy Edition At Home Family Guide** is developed in four pages.

Theme.
Each theme is clearly identified.

Using Our Faith First Books. Each theme is clearly connected to the chapters in the children's **Faith First Legacy Edition** books.

What We Will Learn.
Major aspects of the theme are identified.

Family Blessing. Use this prayer or one of your own to help your family remember God's presence with you.

Photo essay.
This brief, easy-to-read essay gives you background on the theme.

Looking for More? The **Faith First Legacy Edition** program has many additional print, video, and online components. Each will help you and your family learn more about each faith theme. These resources are available online at www.RCLweb.com or by calling 1-877-ASK-4-RCL.

Part 1. The at-home sessions are divided into two meeting or gathering times.

What We Already Know. The theme of the session is introduced and a few moments are spent to discover what the children have already learned and remember about the theme.

What We Will Discover.
The pages in the **Faith First Legacy Edition** student books are identified for the children to read.

THEME 14

Living as the Children of God

The biblical story of creation teaches that God breathed the breath of life into the first human being. This wonderful image reveals the truth of the absolute dependence of humanity on God. Created in God's image and likeness, we are created by God and for God. God's love for us never ceases. God's love for us continually draws us nearer to him.

When we choose to respond to God's love, we choose to live as the children of God. We live as images of God in the world. We announce the good news of God's love to everyone. We are living signs of love and hope.

72 Faith First At Home

Using Our Faith First Legacy Edition Books

Use the following chapters to teach this lesson:
Grade 1 - Chapter 15, see also Chapters 16 and 17
Grade 2 - Chapter 21, see also Chapter 23
Grade 3 - Chapter 21, see also Chapters 4 and 10
Grade 4 - Chapter 18, see also Chapters 19 and 20
Grade 5 - Chapter 20, see also Chapter 21
Grade 6 - Chapter 19, see also Chapter 23

Kindergarten Connection
Faith First Kindergarten Chapters 19 and 21)
Junior High Connection
Faith First Legacy Edition Junior High Morality: Life in Christ Chapters 1, 5, and 8 and Jesus in the New Testament Chapters 8 and 10

What We Will Learn
Through this lesson your family will learn that:
■ God created us to love and know him.
■ Scripture, especially the Beatitudes and the Book of Proverbs and the Book of Psalms, helps us live as children of God.
■ People teach us how to live as the children of God.

Looking for More?
■ www.faithfirst.com
■ **Faith First Legacy Edition** Additional Activities booklet for appropriate age level
■ Faith First videos (Gr. 1—segment 3; Gr. 6—segment 3; Junior High Liturgy and Morality—segment 8)
■ **Faith First Legacy Edition** Called to Prayer booklet for appropriate age level
■ Video Francesco's Friendly World, "The Last Stone"
■ Books to read, see pages 16 and 17

Family Blessing
Loving God,
you created us
in your own image and likeness.
Be with us and bless us
as we learn
how to live as your children.
Amen.

PART 1

What We Already Know
Talk with your children to find out what they already know about living as the children of God. You can begin the discussion by using the example below or your own words.
We believe that we are children of God. What do you think it means to be a child of God?

What We Will Discover
Provide time for the children to read and complete the activities.
Grade 1 Read pages 133–136 to discover why God made us.
Grade 2 Read pages 181–184 to discover how the Proverbs in the Bible help us live as the children of God.
Grade 3 Read pages 181–184 to discover how praying Psalm 104 can help us live as the children of God.
Grade 4 Read pages 157–160 to discover what the Beatitudes tell us about happiness.
Grade 5 Read pages 173–176 to discover how we live holy lives.
Grade 6 Read pages 165–168 to discover how the Spiritual and Corporal Works of Mercy guide us in living holy lives.
Kindergarten Connection
Faith First Kindergarten Chapters 1, 5, and 22
Junior High Connection
Faith First Legacy Edition Junior High Morality: Life in Christ Chapters 1, 5, and 8 and Jesus in the New Testament Chapters 8 and 10

73

Part 2. The second gathering time focuses on group faith sharing and faith decision making.

Sharing Together. The family discusses what the children have learned from their reading. A series of suggested questions is provided to focus the discussion on the main ideas presented in the reading.

What Difference Does Faith Make? This is the heart of the **Faith First** process. Each family member is invited to make a practical, concrete decision to live the faith. The family identifies ways family members can support one another in living out their decisions.

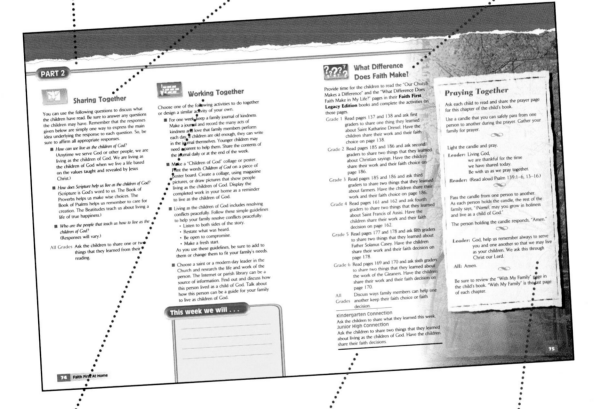

Working Together. Diverse activities are suggested to help each family discover the importance of living what they have learned about the faith.

Kindergarten/Junior High Connection. References to pages in **Faith First Kindergarten** and **Faith First Junior High** are provided for families with children in those grades.

Praying Together. This brief prayer provides the family the opportunity to ask God to bless and help the family and each member of the family to live the faith.

Welcome to Faith First Legacy Edition At Home!

Faith First Legacy Edition At Home Family Guide is a visionary approach to family-guided formation at home. It provides a family-learning and faith-sharing process that respects the schedule demands made on today's families. This program allows you to gather with all your school-age children at the same time and still provide age-appropriate learning.

Faith First Legacy Edition At Home Family Guide provides you with twenty-seven theme sessions designed to be used with your children's **Faith First Legacy Edition** books in an interactive format.

How much time will these lessons take?

You will want to allow between 1 and 1½ hours for each session. You can plan to do each session in a single block of time, or you can divide the session into two shorter sessions. Keep in mind that younger children have a shorter attention span; yet they will require more time for their reading and activities.

How much direction will our children need?

As you begin this program, you will need to provide considerable direction for your children. You will model the example of commitment to this family activity. You will set the prayerful example as you pray together. You will help your children see how important this endeavor

is to all of you. As your children become familiar with the process of the sessions, they will become more willing and able to take more responsibility. Keep in mind that children find security in familiarity. Younger children will continue to require more assistance with the reading than older children will need.

What are some benefits for our family?

The **Faith First Legacy Edition At Home Family Guide** format provides an opportunity for your family to discuss the important things of life. As a parent, you will be sharing your own faith with your children. Faith sharing between parents and children will deepen your relationship with one another and strengthen your faith. You will be learning together. You will hear what is important to your children and what they believe. You will be praying together and getting to know one another better. Your discussions within the sessions will include the shared experience of family life. In a special way, you will be integrating religion and family life each week. As a family you will be setting aside time for something that can be truly valuable for you all.

How can we make these sessions enjoyable for our children?

Invite guests to come and share their stories of faith or ministry. For example, you might invite grandparents, a neighbor who assists in your parish, or perhaps your children's godparents. Children always love to learn from the stories of others. Share stories about your own childhood and childhood faith. Don't just tell the stories of virtue—relate the funny and embarrassing tales as well. Your sessions together should be fun and enjoyable. Don't be afraid to laugh and have a good time. Remember, we refer to the New Testament as the Good News.

How will we assess our progress?

We need to see assessment as an ongoing process and recognize what assessment really is. Assessment is

- a measure of the knowledge acquired.
- a part of all teaching and learning.
- an interactive process between parent and child.
- moving children through different levels of thinking.
- leading children to use knowledge in daily life.
- an opportunity for growth.
- ongoing.

As you can see, you will be assessing progress throughout the **Faith First Legacy Edition At Home** process. The discussions within the sessions—your ongoing dialogue, the questions children ask, how you are praying together, the way you are all engaged in these sessions—all provide assessment of your progress.

If we continue next year, will the material be repetitious?

As you progress through the chapters you will see that although your children of various ages are examining similar themes, they each have their own age-appropriate view of the material. This series is designed around a "spiral model" of education. This means that each year children will revisit a theme such as "Living as the Children of God." Obviously, what a child learns and understands about this theme will vary from first grade to third grade to sixth grade. With regard to the family activities, individual personalities and development will provide plenty of variety!

In what other ways can this program be used?

Faith First Legacy Edition At Home Family Guide can be adapted to almost any group. If your parish has adopted a whole community catechesis model and is developing households of faith, the **At Home Family Guide** gives you just the process you need. In these settings, the program can be used just as it is outlined in this guide.

When used with family clusters, it allows catechists to group the children by similar ages, while not necessitating that they all be of the same age. The catechists can teach as much or as little of each lesson as time allows, and the parents can complete the lesson at home with their children.

In addition, this program can be used as a supplemental resource for parish religion programs or Catholic school programs, allowing teachers to teach the student lesson and families to do the family activities and faith sharing at home.

Free Online Resources

Welcome to www.FaithFirst.com

The award-winning **www.FaithFirst.com** is your family's connection to the new frontier in religious education. With www.FaithFirst.com your family has access to the most innovative and up-to-date Web site available to parents, children, and religious educators today.

Faith First for Families
for parents and children together

- "Just for Parents," a monthly article on parental issues and concerns. Available in both English and Spanish
- "Questions Kids Ask" answers two questions per month that kids most often ask. Available in both English and Spanish
- "Family Prayer," a monthly prayer for family use. Available in both English and Spanish
- "Conversations with Father Bob," a message board moderated by Father Bob Duggan
- "Weekly Bible stories" with adult background
- "Contemporary Issues," a monthly article on adult issues with a Catholic perspective
- "Sunday Gospel Reflections," the readings from the Lectionary that provide reflection and discussion materials for parents and children
- "Make a Difference," ideas for family service activities
- "About Your Child," providing parents with insights into their developing children
- Games for parents and children to do together
- . . . and more

Kids' Clubhouse for Grades K–3
Provides a fun place for primary school age children to visit.

- **Faith First Legacy Edition** chapter-specific activities for children
- Weekly Bible stories
- Weekly saint stories
- "Reading Nook," a continuing story with biweekly installments
- "Chapter Reviews" for grades 1, 2, and 3
- "Tour of a Church"
- "Make a Difference" suggests service activities for children.
- Games
- . . . and more

Kids Only Club for children in grades 4–6

- **Faith First Legacy Edition** chapter-specific activities for children
- "Bible Alive," weekly Scripture stories
- Weekly saint stories
- "River Road Adventures," a weekly interactive serialized story that allows readers to vote to determine how the story will continue
- "Chapter Reviews" for grades 4–6
- "Back in Time," an audio journey back in time to visit with a saint or famous person of faith (close-captioned for hearing impaired)
- "Movie Reviews by Kids," written by youngsters on the latest movies, videos, and CDs
- "Make a Difference," ideas for service activities for youngsters
- Games
- . . . and more

Teen Center for junior high age young people

- **Faith First Legacy Edition** chapter-specific activities for young people
- "Bible Zone," weekly Scripture stories with scriptural background
- Weekly saint stories
- "Vista Falls Junior High," a weekly interactive serialized story that allows readers to vote to determine how the story will continue
- "Chapter Reviews" for junior high
- "Life Timelines," a monthly profile of a saint or person of faith along with a timeline comparison of simultaneous historical events
- "Make a Difference," monthly suggestions for service opportunities
- Games
- . . . and more

Catechists & Teachers

Ideal for parents' use in preparing for **Faith First Legacy Edition At Home Family Guide** sessions, this site includes downloadable activities, blackline masters, current events, sessions for use with the Sunday readings in the Lectionary, plays and skits, and more.

Faith First Videos

Nobody makes videos like RCL! We have produced imaginative and creative videos that

- provide families unique opportunities for faith sharing.
- bring the content of each theme alive visually.

Our **Faith First** videos contain segments on:

- the Bible that transport the children into the life and times of Jesus.

- moral dilemmas that present age-appropriate real-life situations that help the children practice their moral decision-making skills.
- portraits of real-life people who have been transformed by the faith.
- prayer that invite children into a deeper spirituality.
- Bible songs that delight and engage the whole child.
- literature that highlight faith and values with the retelling of original and published stories.

Faith First Grade 1

Segment 1: Bible Songs (5 minutes)—"He's Got the Whole World in His Hands" • "Jesus Loves the Little Children" • "Blessed Be the Name" • "Alleluia"

Segment 2: Bible Songs (5 minutes)—"Come and Go with Me" • "I've Got the Joy" • "Rejoice" • "The Lord Is My Shepherd" • "Whisper a Prayer"

Segment 3: Mrs. Pockets Story (3 minutes)—Mrs. Pockets reads *Plant Your Dreams, My Child* by Gini Bunnell.

Segment 4: Prayer (3 minutes)—Morning Prayer and Evening Prayer with original art and music.

Segment 5: Mrs. Pockets Story (3 minutes)—Mrs. Pockets reads *Mean Soup* by Betsy Everitt.

Segment 6: The Story of St. Nicholas (7 minutes)— Original live-action drama about planning a Christmas play.

Segment 7: Mrs. Pockets Story (3 minutes)—Mrs. Pockets reads *The Wednesday Surprise* by Eve Bunting.

Faith First Grade 2

Segment 1: Bible Songs (6 minutes)—"This Little Light of Mine" • "Alive, Alive" • "Count Your Blessings" • "I've Got Peace Like a River"

Segment 2: Mrs. Pockets Story (12 minutes)—Mrs. Pockets reads *The Clown of God* by Tomie de Paola.

Segment 3: The Story of St. Clare (10 minutes)—Original live-action drama about how Saint Clare shared God's love with others.

Segment 4: Bible Songs (9 minutes)—"This Is the Day" • "Give Me Joy in My Heart" • "This Is My Commandment" • "Lord, I Want to Be a Christian" • "God Is So Good"

Segment 5: Prayer (8 minutes)—Saint Francis's "The Canticle of the Sun" with original art and music.

Segment 6: The Visual Bible™ (8 minutes)—On-location reenactments of the Gospel stories of "The Lost Sheep" • "Call of the First Disciples" • "Blessing of the Children"

Segment 7: The Visual Bible™ (6 minutes)—On-location reenactments of the Gospel story of "The Lord's Supper."

Faith First Grade 3

Segment 1: The Story of St. Patrick (6 minutes)—Original live-action drama about how Saint Patrick used the shamrock to teach that there is one God in three Persons.

Segment 2: The Visual Bible™ (10 minutes)—On-location reenactments of the Gospel stories of "The Preaching of John the Baptist" • "The Baptism of Jesus" • "The Walking on Water."

Segment 3: The Visual Bible™ (7 minutes)—On-location reenactment of the Gospel story of "The Loaves and Fishes."

Segment 4: Moral Dilemma (8 minutes)—Original live-action drama about lying.

Segment 5: Story of Faith (12 minutes)—Actual interviews about volunteer work with the Society for the Prevention of Cruelty to Animals.

Segment 6: Mrs. Pockets Story (12 minutes)—Mrs. Pockets reads *The Easter Story* by Carol Heyer.

Segment 7: Prayer (8 minutes)—The "Our Father" with original art and music.

Faith First Grade 4

Segment 1: Faith First Interview (8 minutes)— Snapshot interviews in which children and teenagers express what faith means to them.

Segment 2: The Visual Bible™ (8 minutes)—On-location reenactment of the Gospel story of "Jesus' Healing Ministry."

Segment 3: Story of Faith (12 minutes)—Actual interview with athlete Jake Repp, who talks about the loss of his leg to cancer and the role of faith in his life.

Segment 4: Moral Dilemma (25 minutes)—Original live-action vignettes that capture day-to-day situations that call us to live the Ten Commandments.

Segment 5: The Visual Bible™ (8 minutes)—On-location reenactment of the Gospel story of "The Sermon on the Mount."

Segment 6: Story of Faith (9 minutes)—Actual interview with teen sisters who organize 400 youth volunteers to serve more than 45 community projects.

Segment 7: Prayer (7 minutes)—"Psalm 148" with original art and music.

Faith First Grade 5

Segment 1: Faith First Interview (8 minutes)—Snapshot interviews in which children and teenagers talk about what faith and prayer mean to them.

Segment 2: The Visual Bible™ (8 minutes)—On-location reenactment of the New Testament story of "The Coming of the Holy Spirit" and "Peter's Speech at Pentecost."

Segment 3: Prayer (4 minutes)—"The Prayer of St. Francis" with original art and music.

Segment 4: Story of Faith (7 minutes)—Interview with Jason Crowe, who raises money for the Cancer Society and for the sculpture "Cellist of Sarejevo."

Segment 5: Moral Dilemma (5 minutes)—Original live-action drama on rumors and false accusations.

Segment 6: Story of Faith (11 minutes)—Interview with Nicole Mason, who organizes teens to renovate rooms in a hospice and to spend time with hospice guests.

Segment 7: The Visual Bible™ (6 minutes)—On-location reenactment of the Gospel story of "Jesus' Teaching on Prayer."

Segment 8: The Visual Bible™ (16 minutes)—On-location reenactment of "The Passion Narrative" in Matthew.

Faith First Grade 6

Segment 1: Faith First Interview (8 minutes)—Snapshot interviews in which children and teenagers talk about the connection between faith and self-esteem.

Segment 2: The Visual Bible™ (6 minutes)—On-location reenactment of the Gospel story of "Ministering to a Great Multitude."

Segment 3: Story of Faith (15 minutes)—Interview with Mark Galvin and his parents, who live in a Catholic Worker homeless shelter.

Segment 4: Moral Dilemma (6 minutes)—Original live-action drama on the consequences of stealing.

Segment 5: Story of Faith (16 minutes)—Interview with the poet Elisa Miranda, who discusses how she finds her identity and expresses her faith through poetry.

Segment 6: The Visual Bible™ (6 minutes)—On-location reenactments of the Gospel stories of "The Judgment of Nations" and "Answers to Prayers."

Segment 7: Prayer (6 minutes)—Original live-action prayer meditations with music.

Segment 8: The Visual Bible™ (18 minutes)—On-location reenactment of "The Passion Narrative" in Matthew.

Faith First Junior High *Creed and Prayer*

Segment 1: Faith First Interview (8 minutes)—Snapshot interviews in which young adults talk about what faith means to them.

Segment 2: The Visual Bible™ (5 minutes)—On-location reenactment of the Gospel story of "The Transfiguration of Jesus."

Segment 3: Social Action (15 minutes)—Interview with Daryle Gentry, who transcended inner-city crime through education and community service.

Segment 4: Story of Faith (15 minutes)—Interviews with students from Columbine High School, who talk about faith and the importance of accepting and respecting others.

Segment 5: Moral Dilemma (6 minutes)—Original live-action drama about cheating.

Segment 6: The Visual Bible™ (18 minutes)—On-location reenactment of "The Passion Narrative" in Matthew.

Segment 7: The Visual Bible™ (8 minutes)—On-location reenactment of the account in the Acts of the Apostles 2–3 of the early mission of the Church in Jerusalem.

Segment 8: Prayer (2 minutes)—Meditation based on Psalm 23, "The Lord Is My Shepherd."

Faith First Junior High *Liturgy and Morality*

Segment 1: Faith First Interview (8 minutes)—Snapshot interviews in which young people talk about the various ways that living their faith makes a difference in their lives.

Segment 2: The Visual Bible™ (8 minutes)—On-location reenactment of the New Testament story of "Pentecost."

Segment 3: Social Action (15 minutes)—Interviews with Sister Helen Prejean and others who are opposed to capital punishment.

Segment 4: Story of Faith (15 minutes)—Interview with Bud Welch, whose daughter was killed in the federal building in Oklahoma City.

Segment 5: Moral Dilemma (8 minutes)—Original live-action drama about a teen party that gets out of control.

Segment 6: The Visual Bible™ (18 minutes)—On-location reenactment of "The Passion Narrative" in Matthew.

Segment 7: The Visual Bible™ (7 minutes)—On-location reenactment of the New Testament account of Saul's (Saint Paul's) conversion.

Segment 8: Prayer (2 minutes)—Meditation based on 1 Corinthians 13, "Paul's Hymn of Love."

Other Resources

Faith First Legacy Edition *Additional Activities* Booklets. Activities for each of the themes to be done by children alone or together with parents. Available for grades 1–6 and junior high.

Faith First Legacy Edition *Called to Prayer* Booklets.
A resource for praying together as a family throughout the year. Available for primary grades (1–3) and intermediate grades (4–6). Each booklet contains morning and evening prayers for Advent, Christmas, Lent, Easter, and Ordinary Time; prayers for holidays; and prayers and blessings for special occasions.

Faith First Legacy Edition *Called to Prayer and Liturgical Lessons* Booklets.
A resource for junior high containing prayers similar to those in the **Called to Prayer** booklets for grades 1–3 and grades 4–6 as well as special liturgical lessons for all the weeks of Advent, Lent, Easter and Pentecost, and the three days of the Easter Triduum.

These resources are available online at www.RCLweb.com or by calling 1-877-ASK-4-RCL.

Resources for Parents

Video

The Mystery of God (Resources for Christian Living). Three thirty-minute videos ("Father," "Jesus," and "Spirit") presenting the basic truths summarized in the creeds of the Church.

Books

Creative Crafts for All Seasons: Projects That Help Kids Learn by Anne Campbell, Kathryn Waite, and Anne Mikelonis (Resources for Christian Living). Engages children of all ages.

Garden of Virtues by Christina Keffler and Rebecca Donnelli, and illustrated by Suzanne Etman (Ave Maria Press). This trio of moms offers 52 ways of teaching children values that will delight you.

Grandparents: Passing On Our Religious Heritage by Marlene Halpin, O.P., Ph.D. (Ave Maria Press). Illuminates ways that grandparents interact with their grandchildren through reading, celebrating, and telling family stories.

Helping Kids Live Their Faith: Service Projects That Make a Difference by Mary Beth Jambor (Resources for Christian Living). Helps children understand the importance of carrying out the Church's mission to serve families, communities, and parish.

How Do I Talk to God? Prayers for the School Year by Barbara Gargiulo (Resources for Christian Living). Presents a unique collection of prayers.

Kids Get Stressed Too: Understanding What's Going On and How to Help by Eileen McGrath, Ph.D. (Resources for Christian Living). Provides ways of teaching kids coping strategies that will last a lifetime.

Spiritual Intelligence by Marsha Sinetar (Orbis Books). Helps parents discover, appreciate, and learn from the inner wisdom of their children and the way children bring to life what is best and most fully human in their hearts.

Teaching Kids the Basics of the Liturgy: Making the Rituals More Meaningful by Robert Duggan (Resources for Christian Living). Explains the Mass and traditions of the Church in simple yet profound terms.

Tend Your Own Garden: How to Raise Great Kids by Timothy E. O'Connell, Ph.D. (Ave Maria Press). There are no guarantees when it comes to raising children. O'Connell offers strategies to help parents encourage their kids to be healthy, happy, and successful.

Catechism of the Catholic Church

(This guide offers easy access to the summary of the Church's teaching of these themes. Numbers indicate paragraph references in the *Catechism*.)

God Our Father and Creator (198–237, 268–300, 325–349)

The Bible, the Word of God (50–133)

Jesus Christ, the Son of God (422–478, 512–560)

The Death and Resurrection of Jesus (571–674, 998–1014, 1020–1050)

The Holy Spirit (683–741, 1091–1109, 1830–1832)

The Church, the People of God (748–801, 811–865, 871–933, 946–959)

Baptism and Confirmation (977–980, 1213–1274, 1285–1314)

Eucharist and the Mass (1322–1405)

Reconciliation and Anointing of the Sick (981–983, 1420–1484, 1499–1525)

Holy Orders and Matrimony (874–896, 1533–1589, 1601–1658)

The Church's Year of Worship (1163–1173)

Loving God (2052–2074, 2083–2132, 2142–2159, 2168–2188)

Loving Others (2196–2246, 2258–2317, 2331–2391, 2401–2449, 2464–2503, 2514–2527, 2534–2550)

Living as the Children of God (1699–1709, 1716–1724, 2447)

Making Choices (1730–1742, 1776–1794, 1846–1869, 1996–2005)

People of Prayer (2558–2589, 2598–2616)

Ways of Praying (2623–2643, 2700–2719, 2746–2751)

The Lord's Prayer (2759–2854)

Mary (484–507, 721–726, 963–972, 2616–2619)

The Parables of Jesus (543, 546, 605, 681, 827, 1038, 1439, 1465, 1696, 1880, 1937, 2607, 2613, 2660, 2707, 2832, 2843)

The Teachings of Jesus (535–556, 1716–1717, 1820)

The Miracles of Jesus (156, 515, 548–549, 1335)

Resources for Children

Bible

The Catholic Youth Bible (St. Mary's Press). Catholic edition of the *New Revised Standard Version (NRSV)*. In addition to containing the complete text of the Bible, it includes 650 lively articles that will help young people pray and live the Bible.

Videos

Blessed Katharine Drexel (Ignatius Press). True story of a woman born into a wealthy family who worked tirelessly to serve American Indians and African Americans and was named a saint in 2000.

Francesco's Friendly World (available from RCL • Resources for Christian Living). Broadcast quality animated videos, each containing ten delightful and enchanting songs. Welcome to Francesco's (Saint Francis of Assisi's) friendly world. It's a happy place where life's simple values are still appreciated and wonderful lessons are taught. Recommended ages 2–9.
  - "The Gifts of Christmas" (44 min.). Celebrate Christmas through songs, suspense, and surprise as Francesco™ begins a Christmas tradition destined to be emulated the world over for centuries to come. The children discover that love outweighs *all* the gifts of Christmas.
  - "The Last Stone" (41 min.). When a storm damages the animals' homes and San Damiano Church, Francesco™ and his friends work together to repair the church before the townspeople arrive at sunrise on Easter morning.

Juan Diego: The Messenger of Guadalupe (Ignatius Press). Tells the story of Our Lady of Guadalupe.

The Perfect Present (Brown-ROA). A girl dreams that she is present at the first Christmas.

Books to Read

The Revelation of God

The Apostles' Creed by Inos Biffi (William B. Eerdmans Publishing Company). Origins and meanings of the Apostles' Creed.

God Loves Me by Julie Walters and Kathryn Kelly (Ave Maria Press). The Psalms introduce children to God's relationship with his people.

Learning to Live in the World by William Stafford (Harcourt Brace and Company). Poems expressing respect for creation.

Jesus and the Church

Christmas Gift: An Anthology of Christmas Poems, Songs, and Stories by Charlemae Hill Rollins (Morrow Junior Books).

Our Church by Graham English (The Liturgical Press). Sharing of religious cultures and customs by children in a multicultural Catholic parish.

The Parables of Jesus by Tomie de Paola (Holiday House, Inc.). A retelling of some of the parables of Jesus.

The Tent: A Parable in One Sitting by Gary Paulsen (Harcourt Brace and Company). The discovery of the meaning of being a disciple.

Worship and Prayer

Birthday Blessings by Bill Freburger (Twenty-Third Publications). Daily prayers come alive through blessings and stories.

Let's Learn About the Church and Celebrate Its Message by Mary Coy Senger (The Liturgical Press). An explanation of the sacraments and Church beliefs.

The Our Father for Children by H. J. Richards (The Liturgical Press). An explanation of the Lord's Prayer.

Our Lady of Guadalupe: Queen of the Americas by Joanne McPortland and Juanita Vaughn (Franciscan Communications). The importance of Mary to the Americas.

The Sacraments by Inos Biffi (William B. Eerdmans Publishing Company). A commentary on the sacraments accompanied by clear, simple pictures.

The Symbols of the Church by Maurice Dilasser (The Liturgical Press). How the Church uses signs and symbols to invite us to deeper worship.

Commandments and Morality

The Empty Pot by Demi (Henry Holt and Company, Inc.). Honesty is the best gift.

Mufaro's Beautiful Daughters by John Steptoe (Lothrop, Lee, and Shepard Books). An African tale that retells the message of Jesus to treat others as they would treat him.

My Life, My Choices by Mary Ann Burkley Wojno (Paulist Press). A useful self-evaluation of key issues that young people face.

Real Heroes Eat Pizza by Tim Hansel (Chariot Victor Books). Children are encouraged to make good choices.

Ten Tips to Help You Get Started

1. Set a schedule when you will meet to work on the program. You might like to invite your children to share their opinions and set up a schedule together. If possible, choose a day of the week and time when you can meet consistently. A regular schedule will be easier to follow.

2. Choose a place to meet. Again, ask your children for their input. Do they prefer to work at a table or would they prefer to sprawl on the floor? However, keep in mind that televisions and telephones can be tempting distractions.

3. With your children, choose some items that you can use for your prayer environment. You might like to use a cloth that changes with the liturgical seasons or the seasons of the calendar year. You will also need a Bible and a candle for prayer. Use a candle that can be passed safely from one family member to another.

4. Choose a place for your family to pray. After completing the work, it is a good idea to change places or postures for prayer. This will help you and your children transition into a prayerful mood. For example, you might work at the kitchen table and then move to the living room for prayer. Or you could sprawl on the floor to work and then sit cross-legged on the floor for prayer.

5. You will need a Bible as you use **Faith First At Home.** We recommend the *New American Bible* or the *New Revised Standard Version, Catholic Edition.*

6. When asking your children for their ideas and responses in each session, remember that there is rarely only one way to express the correct answer. Always make certain that you affirm all the appropriate responses your children offer.

7. Young children will need some assistance when reading and working in their textbooks. You may need to work with them or you could ask an older sibling to help. Take turns reading aloud with young children and offer encouragement as they complete the activities.

8. Do everything possible to eliminate or limit distractions and interruptions. As a family, name and discuss possible interruptions and agree upon how you can avoid them. For example, you may agree not to take phone calls while you are working together.

9. Remember that working with your own children on the **Faith First At Home** program is truly a privilege. By learning together as a family, your family will grow in faith together. Your family's spirituality will be greatly enhanced. You will have opportunities to share important stories together and pray together on a regular basis.

10. In order for your family to experience success with **Faith First At Home** this year, everyone must be committed to one another as well as to the program. Discuss this commitment together as a family. Follow the prayer "Making a Commitment" to ritualize your commitment to learn and grow in faith together.

Checklist

- ❏ Decide when to meet.
- ❏ Choose a place to meet.
- ❏ Locate the items you need for prayer.
- ❏ Choose a place to pray.
- ❏ Make sure you have a Bible.
- ❏ Determine how you can eliminate or limit distractions and interruptions.
- ❏ Make a commitment to one another and to the **Faith First** program.

Making a Commitment

Gather a piece of paper, a pen or pencil, and a piece of ribbon. At the top of the piece of paper write, "We will grow in faith together." Then gather your family together in the place where you have chosen to pray. Set up your prayer cloth, Bible, and candle. Light the candle.

Leader:
Loving God, we thank you for all the blessings that this day has brought to us. We are especially thankful for this opportunity to gather as a family and pray together. We ask you to be with us as we pray.

Reader: (Read aloud Matthew 28:16–20.)

Pass the paper from one person to another. Have each family member sign the paper as a sign of their commitment to the whole family and to growing in faith.

After signing the paper, each person says, "I want to grow in faith!" The other family members respond, "Let us grow in faith together!"

After everyone has signed the paper, roll it up and tie the ribbon around it. Keep the paper with your other prayer items as a reminder of your commitment.

Leader:
Loving God, help us to be faithful to our promise. May our minds and hearts be open to new knowledge and understanding. May the Holy Spirit help us grow in faith and hope and love so that we may live as your children and as followers of your Son, Jesus Christ. We ask this through Christ our Lord.

All: Amen.

God Our Father and Creator

God is the Creator of the universe. All of creation is a generous gift from God. The beauty of creation, the order of the universe, and the diversity and intricacy of all living things tell us that God is good, loving, wonderful, and awesome. In this lesson your family will discover the goodness of God's creation and our call to care for all of creation.

In the Bible there are two stories about creation. Both stories reflect God's love for us. The first creation story is found in chapter one of Genesis. This is the longer of the two stories. The second creation story is found in chapter two of Genesis. It contains the more detailed account of the creation of the first humans.

The biblical stories of creation teach: God created everything, and everything God created is good; the pinnacle of creation was the creation of human beings in God's own image; God asked humankind to care for creation.

Using Our Faith First Legacy Edition Books

Use the following chapters to teach this lesson:

Grade 1 · Chapter 2
Grade 2 · Chapter 3
Grade 3 · Chapter 2
Grade 4 · Chapter 4
Grade 5 · Chapter 5
Grade 6 · Chapter 4

Kindergarten Connection
Faith First Kindergarten
Chapters 2 and 7
Junior High Connection
Faith First Legacy Edition Junior High
Mystery of God Chapters 1, 4, and 5

What We Will Learn

Through this lesson your family will learn that:

- God created the world and that everything God created is good.
- God created people in his own image and likeness.
- Jesus taught us to call God our Father.
- We show our love for God when we take care of creation.

Looking for More?

- **www.FaithFirst.com**
- **Faith First Legacy Edition** *Additional Activities* booklet for appropriate age level
- **Faith First** videos (Grade 2—segment 5; Grade 4—segment 7; Junior High *Creed and Prayer*—segment 8)
- **Faith First Legacy Edition** *Called to Prayer* booklet for appropriate age level
- Books to read, see pages 16 and 17

Family Blessing

Loving God,
Creator of the universe,
we ask for your blessing upon us.
Help us remember that
you have created each of us
in your image and likeness.
Amen.

PART 1

What We Already Know

Talk with your children to find out what they already know about God and creation. You can begin the discussion by using the example below or your own words.

We believe that God created the universe. Let's share with one another what each of us likes best in all of creation.

What We Will Discover

Provide time for the children to read and complete the activities.

Grade 1   Read pages 21–24 to discover one way we can show our love for God.

Grade 2   Read pages 29–32 to discover why we call God our Father.

Grade 3   Read pages 21–24 to discover how creation helps us know that God loves us.

Grade 4   Read pages 37–40 to discover why human beings are the greatest of all God's creation.

Grade 5   Read pages 45–48 to discover four names we use for God and the special name Jesus uses for God.

Grade 6   Read pages 37–40 to discover what we mean when we say that God created the world and created us in his own image and likeness.

Kindergarten Connection
Faith First Kindergarten Chapters 2 and 7
Junior High Connection
Faith First Legacy Edition Junior High *Mystery of God*
Chapters 1, 4, and 5

Sharing Together

You can use the following questions to discuss what the children have read. Be sure to answer any questions the children may have. Remember that the responses given below are simply one way to express the main idea underlying the response to each question, so be sure to affirm all appropriate responses.

- *What do we mean when we say that God created the world and made us in his own image?*
  (God created us to be like him.)

- *Why are human beings the greatest of all God's creation?*
  (Humans are the greatest because we are created in the image and likeness of God.)

- *How does creation help us know that God cares for us?*
  (The beauty and wonderful things in creation tell us of God's goodness and his love for us.)

- *What are some names that we use for God?*
  (We call God Almighty, Creator, Father, Truth, Love, One, Holy, and Eternal.)

- *What is Jesus' special name for God?*
  (Jesus called God Abba, or Father.)

- *Why do we call God our Father?*
  (God created us and we are children of God. Jesus taught us to call God our Father.)

- *How can we show our love for God?*
  (We can show our love for God by taking care of creation.)

All Grades Ask the children to share one or two things that they learned from their reading.

Working Together

Choose one of the following activities to do together or design a similar activity of your own.

- Look at baby pictures of each family member. Have family members take turns telling each other what they like about how God created each family member.

- Have someone read aloud the creation story from Genesis 1:1–2:3. (Read from a Bible, a children's Bible, or page 30 of the **Faith First Legacy Edition** Grade 2 book.) As one person reads this passage, ask everyone else to pretend to be the various parts of creation as God creates them. For example, when the reader reads that God created animals, each person will pretend to be an animal.

- Go for a walk and name the gifts of creation that you can see, hear, smell, taste, and touch. Thank God for all these wonderful gifts!

- List a number of ways your family can take care of God's creation. Create a family plan to take care of one aspect of creation or make posters or videotape skits that encourage people to care for creation.

This week we will . . .

_____
_____
_____
_____
_____
_____
_____
_____
_____
_____

What Difference Does Faith Make?

Provide time for the children to read the "Our Church Makes a Difference" and the "What Difference Does Faith Make in My Life?" pages in their **Faith First Legacy Edition** books and complete the activities on those pages.

Grade 1 Read pages 25 and 26 and ask first graders to share one thing they learned about the "Adopt-a-Street" program. Have the children share their work and their faith choice on page 26.

Grade 2 Read pages 33 and 34 and ask second graders to share two things that they learned about Saint Augustine. Have the children share their work and their faith choice on page 34.

Grade 3 Read pages 25 and 26 and ask third graders to share two things that they learned about creation and their parish. Have the children share their work and their faith choice on page 26.

Grade 4 Read pages 41 and 42 and ask fourth graders to share two things that they learned about Saints Isidore and Maria and how these saints showed they believed that God is the Creator. Have the children share their work and their faith decision on page 42.

Grade 5 Read pages 49 and 50 and ask fifth graders to share two things that they learned about blessings and prayers. Have the children share their work and their faith decision on page 50.

Grade 6 Read pages 41 and 42 and ask sixth graders to share two things that they learned about mosaics. Have the children share their work and their faith decision on page 42.

All Grades Discuss ways family members can help one another keep their faith choice or faith decision.

Kindergarten Connection
Ask the children to share what they learned this week.
Junior High Connection
Ask the children to share two things that they learned about God. Have the children share their faith decisions.

Praying Together

Ask each child to read and share the prayer page for this chapter of the child's book.

Give everyone a minute or two to find an object in your home that symbolizes a gift of creation for which they are thankful. Gather the group for prayer.

Light a candle and pray.

Leader: God our Creator,
we are thankful for the time
we have shared today.
Be with us as we pray together.

Ask each person to present their object and say, "I am thankful for _____." After each person speaks, the rest of the family responds, "*(Name)*, you are created in God's image. May God bless you as you take care of creation."

Leader: God, help us remember to always give thanks for the many gifts of creation and to take care of everything you have created for us to enjoy. We ask this through Christ our Lord.

All: Amen.

Be sure to review the "With My Family" page in the child's book. "With My Family" is the last page of each chapter.

The Bible, the Word of God

To understand the importance of the Bible in our life of faith, we need to understand the phrase "the word of God." As Catholics, we believe that the word of God, Sacred Scripture, is God's communication of himself to all people. We also believe that all the human writers of Sacred Scripture were inspired by the Holy Spirit. These writers used a variety of genres, such as poetry, songs, narratives, and parables, to communicate God's word to us.

Two principles can help us understand the meaning of Sacred Scripture and discuss this meaning within our family. First, we need to consider the times and culture of each writer in order to find out what the writer is trying to convey about God. Second, we need to respect the unity of Sacred Scripture. This means that we must always read each passage, chapter, and book with regard to the entire Bible.

Using Our Faith First Legacy Edition Books

Use the following chapters to teach this lesson:

Grade 1 · Chapter 1

Grade 2 · Chapter 1

Grade 3 · Chapter 1

Grade 4 · Chapter 2

Grade 5 · Chapter 2

Grade 6 · Chapter 2

Kindergarten Connection
Faith First Kindergarten Chapter 6
Junior High Connection
Faith First Legacy Edition Junior High
Mystery of God Chapter 2 and *Jesus in the New Testament* Chapters 1 and 2

What We Will Learn

Through this lesson your family will learn that:

■ Stories in the Bible help us know God.

■ The Church helps us know God.

■ Family members teach one another about God.

■ The word of God affects our lives.

Looking for More?

■ **www.FaithFirst.com**

■ **Faith First Legacy Edition** *Additional Activities* booklets for appropriate age level

■ **Faith First** videos (Grade 1—segments 1, 2; Grade 2—segments 1, 4; Grade 3—segments 2, 3, 8; Grade 4—segments 2, 5, 7; Grade 5—segments 2, 7; Grade 6—segments 2, 6, 8; Junior High *Creed and Prayer*—segments 2, 6, 7, 8; *Liturgy and Morality*—segments 2, 6, 7, 8)

■ **Faith First Legacy Edition** *Called to Prayer* booklet for appropriate age level

■ Books to read, see pages 16 and 17

Family Blessing

Loving God,
bless and be with our family.
Help us to love your word
and to always listen
when you speak to us.
Amen.

PART 1

What We Already Know

Talk with your children to find out what they already know about how we learn about God. You can begin the discussion by using the example below or your own words.

We believe that we learn about God from stories in the Bible, from the Church, and from the people we know. Let's share with one another what each of us has learned about God from the Bible, from the Church, and from people.

What We Will Discover

Provide time for the children to read and complete the activities.

Grade 1   Read pages 13–16 to discover what the Bible story about Abraham and Sarah tells us about God.

Grade 2   Read pages 13–16 to discover what Jesus tells us about God.

Grade 3   Read pages 13–16 to discover some ways that God speaks to us.

Grade 4   Read pages 21–24 to discover why the four accounts of the Gospel are the heart of the New Testament.

Grade 5   Read pages 21–24 to discover what the writings of the New Testament teach us.

Grade 6   Read pages 21–24 to discover how God reveals himself through the Bible.

Kindergarten Connection
Faith First Kindergarten Chapter 6
Junior High Connection
Faith First Legacy Edition Junior High *Mystery of God* Chapter 2 and *Jesus in the New Testament* Chapters 1 and 2

Sharing Together

You can use the following questions to discuss what the children have read. Be sure to answer any questions the children may have. Remember that the responses given below are simply one way to express the main idea underlying the response to each question, so be sure to affirm all appropriate responses.

- *How does the Bible tell us about God?*
  (The Bible is God's own word to us. It is the inspired written word of God. By reading or listening to stories from the Bible, we learn about God.)

- *What does Jesus tell us about God?*
  (Jesus tells us about God's love for us.)

- *How does our family help us know and love God?*
  (Our family prays together and talks about God.)

- *How does our parish community help us know and love God?*
  (The people in our parish help us learn about God. They share God's love with one another by helping each other. They pray and worship together.)

- *Who are some people who have taught us about God?*
  (Responses will vary.)

All Grades Ask the children to share one or two things that they learned from their reading.

Working Together

Choose one of the following activities to do together or design a similar activity of your own.

- Make a list of everyone's favorite Bible stories. Invite each person to make an illustration for his or her story. Share with each other what each story tells us about God.

- Choose a story from the Bible and act it out. You can use some items from around your home to make costumes. Talk about what your family has learned about God from the story.

- Go to a bookstore or religious gift store and look at all the different types of Bibles. Talk about who might use each type of Bible.

- Think of all the people who have helped you know and love God. Make thank-you cards and send them to these people.

- If you have a family Bible, you might display it in a special place in your home to help your family remember the importance of God's word.

This week we will . . .

_____

_____

_____

_____

_____

_____

_____

_____

_____

What Difference Does Faith Make?

Provide time for the children to read the "Our Church Makes a Difference" and the "What Difference Does Faith Make in My Life?" pages in their **Faith First Legacy Edition** books and complete the activities on those pages.

Grade 1 Read pages 17 and 18 and ask first graders to share one thing they learned about a parish. Have the children share their faith choice on page 18.

Grade 2 Read pages 17 and 18 and ask second graders to share two things that they learned about parish communities. Have the children share their work and their faith choice on page 18.

Grade 3 Read pages 17 and 18 and ask third graders to share two things that they learned about Christian art. Have the children share their work and their faith choice on page 18.

Grade 4 Read pages 25 and 26 and ask fourth graders to share two things that they learned about the Bible. Have the children share their work and their faith decision on page 26.

Grade 5 Read pages 25 and 26 and ask fifth graders to share two things that they learned about reverence for the Bible. Have the children share their work and their faith decision on page 26.

Grade 6 Read pages 25 and 26 and ask sixth graders to share two things that they learned about Scripture services. Have the children share their work and their faith decision on page 26.

All Grades Discuss ways family members can help one another keep their faith choice or faith decision.

Kindergarten Connection
Ask the children to share what they learned this week.
Junior High Connection
Ask the children to share two things that they learned about Sacred Scripture. Have the children share their faith decisions.

Praying Together

Ask each child to read and share the prayer page for this chapter of the child's book.

Invite everyone to think of a person who has helped them know and love God. After a few moments of silent reflection, gather your family for prayer.

Light a candle, place a Bible next to the candle, and pray.
Leader: God our Creator,
we are thankful for the time
we have shared today.
Be with us as we pray together.

Pass the Bible from one family member to another. As each person holds the Bible, ask them to share the name of a person who has helped them come to know and love God, saying, "God, I thank you for _____." After each petition, have the rest of the family respond, "Lord, help us know you and love you."

Leader: God, help us find you in the Bible, in the Church, and in other people.
Help us always listen when you speak.
We ask this through Christ our Lord.
All: Amen.

Be sure to review the "With My Family" page in the child's book. "With My Family" is the last page of each chapter.

Jesus Christ, the Son of God

The mystery of the Incarnation—the fact that the Son of God became human without giving up his divinity, reveals the infinite love of God for us. Jesus Christ is true God and true man. In him God's promises are fulfilled. Jesus' whole life on earth proclaimed God's love and care for all of us.

For most of his life on earth, Jesus was not a recognized public figure. He lived a life similar to that of most of his contemporaries and gave little evidence of his greatness. He lived in Nazareth, obeyed Mary and Joseph, and observed the laws and traditions of the Jewish religion. After John baptized Jesus in the Jordan River, Jesus began his public life and ministry. All Jesus' deeds and words reveal God's saving love and invite us to follow him and become his disciples.

Jesus is a model for our holiness. Through the example of his own loving-kindness, Jesus showed us how to love God and one another. The Holy Spirit invites us to learn from Jesus' life and teachings. The Holy Spirit encourages us to pray as Jesus prayed.

Using Our Faith First Legacy Edition Books

Use the following chapters to teach this lesson:

Grade 1 · Chapter 3

Grade 2 · Chapter 5, see also chapter 6

Grade 3 · Chapter 5

Grade 4 · Chapter 6, see also chapter 5

Grade 5 · Chapter 6

Grade 6 · Chapter 5

Kindergarten Connection
Faith First Kindergarten Chapters 10 and 12
Junior High Connection
Faith First Legacy Edition Junior High *Mystery of God* Chapters 6 and 7

What We Will Learn

Through this lesson your family will learn that:

- Jesus is the Son of God.
- Jesus' family is called the Holy Family.
- Jesus tells us about God's love.
- Jesus teaches us to love and serve God and others.

Looking for More?

- **www.FaithFirst.com**
- **Faith First Legacy Edition** *Additional Activities* booklet for appropriate age level
- **Faith First** videos (Grade 3— segment 2; Grade 4—segment 5; Grade 6—segments 2, 6; Junior High *Creed and Prayer*—segment 2)
- **Faith First Legacy Edition** *Called to Prayer* booklet for appropriate age level
- Books to read, see pages 16 and 17

Family Blessing

God the Father of all,
bless our family
as we learn about your Son,
the Promised One, Jesus.
Amen.

PART 1

What We Already Know

Talk with your children to find out what they already know about Jesus, the Son of God. You can begin the discussion by using the example below or your own words.

We believe that Jesus is the Son of God. Let's each share a story about Jesus that we remember from the Bible.

What We Will Discover

Provide time for the children to read and complete the activities.

Grade 1   Read pages 29–32 to discover a story about Jesus and his family.

Grade 2   Read pages 45–48 to discover what God's promise was.

Grade 3   Read pages 45–48 to discover the Good News that Jesus announced.

Grade 4   Read pages 53–56 to discover how Jesus showed that he was God's Promised One.

Grade 5   Read pages 53–56 to discover three titles that we use for Jesus.

Grade 6   Read pages 45–48 to discover what the Church believes about Jesus.

Kindergarten Connection
Faith First Kindergarten Chapters 10 and 12
Junior High Connection
Faith First Legacy Edition Junior High *Mystery of God* Chapters 6 and 7

Sharing Together

You can use the following questions to discuss what the children have read. Be sure to answer any questions the children may have. Remember that the responses given below are simply one way to express the main idea underlying the response to each question, so be sure to affirm all appropriate responses.

■ *What was God's promise?*
(God promised to send someone to help his people. God promised to send a messiah or savior.)

■ *Who is the Holy Family?*
(The Holy Family is Jesus, Mary, and Joseph.)

■ *What did Jesus do to show us how to live?*
(Jesus taught us to love and serve God and others. Jesus treated everyone with love, respect, and kindness.)

■ *How did Jesus show God's love for us?*
(Jesus showed God's love for us by caring for people. Jesus showed God's love for us by saving us from our sins.)

■ *How does our family follow Jesus?*
(Responses will vary.)

All Grades Ask the children to share one or two things that they learned from their reading.

Working Together

Choose one of the following activities to do together or design a similar activity of your own.

■ First, list the ways that your family follows Jesus. Then make a mural illustrating the ways that your family follows Jesus.

■ Act out the story of Jesus' birth. Read Luke 2:1–20 or page 47 of the **Faith First Legacy Edition** Grade 2 book. Afterward, ask the children to share what the character they acted out knew about Jesus.

■ Look in books or visit your church to find statues and paintings of Jesus. Talk about what each piece of art tells about Jesus.

■ Watch the news or look in the newspaper for examples of people who are helping others. Discuss how these people are doing what Jesus taught us to do.

This week we will . . .

What Difference Does Faith Make?

Provide time for the children to read the "Our Church Makes a Difference" and the "What Difference Does Faith Make in My Life?" pages in their **Faith First Legacy Edition** books and complete the activities on those pages.

Grade 1 Read pages 33 and 34 and ask first graders to share one thing they learned about the Church. Have the children share their work and their faith choice on page 34.

Grade 2 Read pages 49 and 50 and ask second graders to share two things that they learned about the Church. Have the children share their work and their faith choice on page 50.

Grade 3 Read pages 49 and 50 and ask third graders to share two things that they learned about the Good News in action. Have the children share their work and their faith choice on page 50.

Grade 4 Read pages 57 and 58 and ask fourth graders to share two things that they learned about how patron saints help us live as followers of Jesus. Have the children share their work and their faith decision on page 58.

Grade 5 Read pages 57 and 58 and ask fifth graders to share two things that they learned about sacred art. Have the children share their work and their faith decision on page 58.

Grade 6 Read pages 49 and 50 and ask sixth graders to share two things that they learned about the Passionists. Have the children share their work and their faith decision on page 50.

All Grades Discuss ways family members can help one another keep their faith choice or faith decision.

Kindergarten Connection
Ask the children to share what they learned this week.

Junior High Connection
Ask the children to share two things that they learned about Jesus. Have the children share their faith decisions.

Praying Together

Ask each child to read and share the prayer page for this chapter of the child's book.

Find a religious object or create a paper cross to use during your family prayer time. Then gather your family for prayer.

Light a candle and pray.

Leader: God our Creator,
we are thankful for the time
we have shared today.
Be with us as we pray together.

Each person, one at a time, holds the cross or religious object. Have the rest of the family members take turns naming why they are thankful for the family member holding the cross. Each family member will say, "God, I am thankful for _____ because _____." After each petition, the whole family responds together, "Help us to be like the Holy Family and to follow Jesus."

Leader: Father in heaven, we give you thanks and praise for our family. Bless us and help us show our love for you and for one another as the Holy Family did. We ask this in the name of your Son, Jesus Christ.

All: Amen.

Be sure to review the "With My Family" page in the child's book. "With My Family" is the last page of each chapter.

The Death and Resurrection of Jesus

From the beginning of his public ministry Jesus challenged the religious leaders of his day to think about the true meaning of the Covenant that God had made with his people. Jesus expelled demons and forgave sins. Jesus healed on the Sabbath. He challenged the triviality of the endless number of man-made laws by preaching the Law of Love.

Jesus' teachings and actions eventually led to his Passion and death. The suffering of Jesus was not without purpose. Though Jesus was without sin, he suffered willingly for all of us. In accepting his death on a cross, Jesus placed his life in complete conformity with the divine plan. His Resurrection opened the way for us to new life. Joined to Christ and his death and Resurrection through our Baptism, we share in the Paschal Mystery and are empowered to live our new life in Christ.

Using Our Faith First Legacy Edition Books

Use the following chapters to teach this lesson:

Grade 1 · Chapter 5
Grade 2 · Chapter 7
Grade 3 · Chapter 6
Grade 4 · Chapter 7
Grade 5 · Chapter 7
Grade 6 · Chapter 5, pages 48–49

Kindergarten Connection
Faith First Kindergarten Chapter 13
Junior High Connection
Faith First Legacy Edition Junior High
Mystery of God Chapters 8, 9, 10, and 11

What We Will Learn

Through this lesson your family will learn that:

- Jesus suffered and died.
- Jesus was raised from the dead and ascended to his Father.
- The Paschal Mystery is the mystery of Jesus' Passion, death, Resurrection, and Ascension.
- We live our faith in the Paschal Mystery.

Looking for More?

- **www.FaithFirst.com**
- **Faith First Legacy Edition** *Additional Activities* booklet for appropriate age level
- **Faith First** videos (Grade 3— segment 6; Grade 5—segment 8; Grade 6—segment 8; Junior High *Creed and Prayer*—segment 6; *Liturgy and Morality*—segment 6)
- **Faith First Legacy Edition** *Called to Prayer* booklet for appropriate age level
- Books to read, see pages 16 and 17

Family Blessing

*God our loving Father,
we ask you to bless and be with
our family as we learn more
about the death and Resurrection
of your Son, our Lord Jesus Christ.
Amen.*

PART 1

What We Already Know

Talk with your children to find out what they already know about Jesus' suffering, death, Resurrection, and Ascension. You can begin the discussion by using the example below or your own words.

We believe that Jesus died on a cross, was raised to new life, and returned to his Father in heaven. What do you already know about these events?

What We Will Discover

Provide time for the children to read and complete the activities.

Grade 1   Read pages 45–48 to discover what the Paschal Mystery of Jesus is.

Grade 2   Read pages 62–67 to discover what the Resurrection is.

Grade 3   Read pages 53–56 to discover what the Paschal Mystery tells us about God's love.

Grade 4   Read pages 61–64 to discover what happened at Jesus' trial and death.

Grade 5   Read pages 61–64 to discover what the Paschal Mystery of Jesus is.

Grade 6   Read pages 45–48 to discover why the death and Resurrection of Jesus is so important.

Kindergarten Connection
Faith First Kindergarten Chapter 13
Junior High Connection
Faith First Legacy Edition Junior High *Mystery of God* Chapters 8, 9, 10, and 11

Sharing Together

You can use the following questions to discuss what the children have read. Be sure to answer any questions the children may have. Remember that the responses given below are simply one way to express the main idea underlying the response to each question, so be sure to affirm all appropriate responses.

- *What happened at Jesus' trial and death?*
  (Pilate sentenced Jesus to death by crucifixion. Jesus was nailed to the cross and died on the cross.)

- *What happened three days after Jesus died?*
  (The tomb was empty. Jesus was raised from the dead. This is the Resurrection.)

- *What is the Resurrection?*
  (The Resurrection is Jesus rising from the dead on the third day after his death and burial.)

- *How does the crucifix remind us of Jesus?*
  (A crucifix has an image of Jesus' body on it. It reminds us that Jesus died on a cross.)

- *What is the Ascension?*
  (The Ascension is the return of the Risen Jesus to his Father in heaven.)

All Grades Ask the children to share one or two things that they learned from their reading.

Working Together

Choose one of the following activities to do together or design a similar activity of your own.

- Visit your church and pray the Stations of the Cross. Afterward, talk about how the Stations of the Cross tell the story of Jesus' Passion and death.

- Visit a few Catholic churches in your area and look at the Stations of the Cross. Compare the sacred art. Talk about how each set of Stations tells the story in a unique manner.

- The next time you take part in Mass, notice all the words and symbols of Jesus' death and Resurrection. After Mass share what you noticed with one another to discover the ways we remember Jesus' death and Resurrection during Mass.

- At Mass we pray aloud or sing the memorial acclamation "Christ has died, Christ is risen, Christ will come again." Throughout the week, sing together a memorial acclamation whenever you pray together as a family. You can use an acclamation melody sung by your parish or put the words to your own melody.

This week we will . . .

_____

_____

_____

_____

_____

_____

_____

_____

_____

What Difference Does Faith Make?

Provide time for the children to read the "Our Church Makes a Difference" and the "What Difference Does Faith Make in My Life?" pages in their **Faith First Legacy Edition** books and complete the activities on those pages.

Grade 1 Read pages 49 and 50 and ask first graders to share one thing that they learned about the Church's use of candles. Have the children share their work and their faith choice on page 50.

Grade 2 Read pages 65 and 66 and ask second graders to share two things that they learned about the Easter candle. Have the children share their work and their faith choice on page 66.

Grade 3 Read pages 57 and 58 and ask third graders to share two things that they learned about the Way of the Cross, or the Stations of the Cross. Have the children share their work and their faith choice on page 58.

Grade 4 Read pages 65 and 66 and ask fourth graders to share two things that they learned about Saint Helena. Have the children share their work and their faith decision on page 66.

Grade 5 Read pages 65 and 66 and ask fifth graders to share two things that they learned about the Stations of the Cross. Have the children share their work and their faith decision on page 66.

Grade 6 Read pages 49 and 50 and ask sixth graders to share two things that they learned about Saint Paul of the Cross and the Passionists. Have the children share their work and their faith decision on page 50.

All Grades Discuss ways family members can help one another keep their faith choice or faith decision.

Kindergarten Connection
Ask the children to share what they learned this week.

Junior High Connection
Ask the children to share two things that they learned about the death and Resurrection of Jesus. Have the children share their faith decisions.

Praying Together

Ask each child to read and share the prayer page for this chapter of the child's book.

Find a crucifix to use during your family prayer time. If you do not have one available, create a cross out of paper. Then gather your family for prayer.

Light a candle and pray.

Leader: God our Creator,
we are thankful for the time
we have shared today.
Be with us as we pray together.

Reader: (Read aloud Luke 24:1–12.)

Pass the cross or crucifix from person to person and invite each person as they hold it to say, "Jesus is with me."

After each statement, invite the whole family to respond, "Alleluia!"

Leader: Jesus, the depth of your love for us is overwhelming. You gave your life for us. May our lives lead others to discover your love for them. In your name we pray.

All: Amen.

Be sure to review the "With My Family" page in the child's book. "With My Family" is the last page of each chapter.

The Holy Spirit

The Scriptures tell us that Jesus' followers were filled with the Holy Spirit when they were gathered in the upper room in Jerusalem fifty days after the Ascension on the Jewish feast of Pentecost. That event, which includes the manifestation of the Holy Spirit in a strong wind and tongues of fire, empowered the disciples to proclaim the Good News. Inspired by the Holy Spirit, the disciples followed Jesus' command to take his mission into the world.

The Holy Spirit sparks faith in the hearts of all who believe in Jesus Christ. We come to know and believe in Christ through the power of the Holy Spirit. The Holy Spirit is our guide, our teacher, our advocate, our helper. The Holy Spirit blesses us with gifts and empowers us to live as followers of Jesus.

Using Our Faith First Legacy Edition Books

Use the following chapters to teach this lesson:

Grade 1 · Chapter 7

Grade 2 · Chapter 9

Grade 3 · Chapter 7

Grade 4 · Chapter 8

Grade 5 · Chapter 8, see also chapters 9 and 13

Grade 6 · Chapter 7

Kindergarten Connection
Faith First Kindergarten Chapter 18
Junior High Connection
Faith First Legacy Edition Junior High
Mystery of God Chapter 12, and *Morality:*
Life in Christ Chapter 6

What We Will Learn

Through this lesson your family will learn that:

■ The Holy Trinity is God the Father, God the Son, and God the Holy Spirit.

■ Jesus, the Son of God, promised that God the Father and he would send the Holy Spirit.

■ The Holy Spirit came to Jesus' followers on Pentecost.

■ The Holy Spirit helps us live as followers of Jesus Christ.

Looking for More?

■ **www.FaithFirst.com**

■ **Faith First Legacy Edition** *Additional Activities* booklet for appropriate age level

■ **Faith First** videos (Grade 3— segment 1; Grade 5—segment 2; Junior High *Liturgy and Morality*— segment 2)

■ **Faith First Legacy Edition** *Called to Prayer* booklet for appropriate age level

■ Books to read, see pages 16 and 17

Family Blessing

Spirit of God,
who came in wind and fire,
fill our hearts with courage
and strength.
Help us grow closer to you.
Amen.

PART 1

 ## What We Already Know

Talk with your children to find out what they already know about the Holy Spirit. You can begin the discussion by using the example below or your own words.

We believe that God the Holy Spirit is our helper and guide. What do you know about the Holy Spirit?

 ## What We Will Discover

Provide time for the children to read and complete the activities.

Grade 1 Read pages 61–64 to discover how the Holy Spirit helps us.

Grade 2 Read pages 77–80 to discover why God the Father and Jesus, God the Son, sent us the Holy Spirit.

Grade 3 Read pages 61–64 to discover how the Holy Spirit helped the disciples who were gathered in the upper room.

Grade 4 Read pages 69–72 to discover what happened on Pentecost.

Grade 5 Read pages 69–72 to discover how the Holy Spirit helps us.

Grade 6 Read pages 61–64 to discover what the four marks of the Church tell about the Church.

Kindergarten Connection
Faith First Kindergarten Chapter 18
Junior High Connection
Faith First Legacy Edition Junior High *Mystery of God* Chapter 12 and *Morality: Life in Christ* Chapter 6

Sharing Together

You can use the following questions to discuss what the children have read. Be sure to answer any questions the children may have. Remember that the responses given below are simply one way to express the main idea underlying the response to each question, so be sure to affirm all appropriate responses.

- *Who is the Holy Trinity?*
  (The Holy Trinity is the mystery of the one God in three divine Persons: God the Father, God the Son, God the Holy Spirit.)

- *Who did God the Father and Jesus, God the Son, send to help us?* (Jesus promised that he and the Father would send the Holy Spirit.)

- *Why was the Holy Spirit sent to us?*
  (The Holy Spirit was sent to be our helper and guide.)

- *How does the Holy Spirit help us?*
  (The Holy Spirit helps us keep Jesus' memory alive and understand what Jesus taught and did. The Holy Spirit helps us live as followers of Jesus.)

- *What happened on Pentecost?*
  (The Holy Spirit came to Jesus' followers. The Holy Spirit helped the disciples to continue Jesus' mission and to spread the Good News.)

All Grades Ask the children to share one or two things that they learned from their reading.

Working Together

Choose one of the following activities to do together or design a similar activity of your own.

- The Holy Spirit is our helper. Make a list of ways you can help one another. Invite each person to put a star by one thing that they will do this week.

- Read John 14:15–30. Discuss how the Holy Spirit helps your family live as a Christian family.

- List ways the Holy Spirit helps your family. Post the list on the refrigerator or in a place where everyone will see it. Mark a check next to the things on the list as they occur this week.

- Read aloud the definition of the word *advocate* from a dictionary. Create a list of family members and friends whom you see as being advocates in some way. Identify how the Holy Spirit might be helping these people be advocates to help others live as followers of Jesus.

This week we will . . .

_____

_____

_____

_____

_____

_____

_____

_____

_____

What Difference Does Faith Make?

Provide time for the children to read the "Our Church Makes a Difference" and the "What Difference Does Faith Make in My Life?" pages in their **Faith First Legacy Edition** books and complete the activities on those pages.

Grade 1 Read pages 65 and 66 and ask first graders to share one thing that they learned about signs of the Holy Spirit. Have the children share their work and their faith choice on page 66.

Grade 2 Read pages 81 and 82 and ask second graders to share two things that they learned about Pentecost. Have the children share their work and their faith choice on page 82.

Grade 3 Read pages 65 and 66 and ask third graders to share two things that they learned about signs of the Holy Spirit. Have the children share their work and their faith choice on page 66.

Grade 4 Read pages 73 and 74 and ask fourth graders to share two things that they learned about missionaries. Have the children share their work and their faith decision on page 74.

Grade 5 Read pages 73 and 74 and ask fifth graders to share two things that they learned about hymns. Have the children share their work and their faith decision on page 74.

Grade 6 Read pages 65 and 66 and ask sixth graders to share two things that they learned about letters from the Church. Have the children share their work and their faith decision on page 66.

All Grades Discuss ways family members can help one another keep their faith choice or faith decision.

Kindergarten Connection
Ask the children to share what they learned this week.

Junior High Connection
Ask the children to share two things that they learned about the Holy Spirit. Have the children share their faith decisions.

Praying Together

Ask each child to read and share the prayer page for this chapter of the child's book.

For prayer today, use a candle that can be passed safely from person to person. Then gather your family for prayer.

Light a candle and pray.

Leader: Loving God,
we are thankful for the time
we have shared today.
Be with us as we pray together.

Pass a candle from person to person. As each person holds the candle everyone else says together, "*(Name)*, the Holy Spirit is your helper and guide." The person holding the candle responds, "Amen."

Leader: Come, Holy Spirit; fill the hearts of your faithful ones. Help us remember to look to you for guidance. Bless us with your many gifts. We ask this through Christ our Lord.

All: Amen.

Be sure to review the "With My Family" page in the child's book. "With My Family" is the last page of each chapter.

The Church, the People of God

The Church is the People of God and the Body of Christ. The Church is the Communion of Saints—the faithful alive on earth and the faithful who have died, the community of the followers of Jesus who are in relationship with one another.

We, the Church, make Christ visible, continue his mission, and are signs of Christ in the world. Through the community of the Church our faith is nurtured and flourishes. As members of the Church we give witness to Christ by our love, kindness, and unity. Together as a community, we strive for a deepening of faith and conversion so that our lives will be clearer images of Christ as we serve God's plan, continue Jesus' work in the world, and prepare for the coming of the kingdom of God.

Using Our Faith First Legacy Edition Books

Use the following chapters to teach this lesson:

Grade 1 · Chapter 8

Grade 2 · Chapter 10

Grade 3 · Chapter 8

Grade 4 · Chapter 10

Grade 5 · Chapter 10

Grade 6 · Chapter 8, see also chapter 14

Kindergarten Connection
Faith First Kindergarten
Chapters 9 and 17
Junior High Connection
Faith First Legacy Edition Junior High
Church and Sacraments Chapters 1 and 2

What We Will Learn

Through this lesson your family will learn that:

■ The Church is the People of God.

■ As members of the Church, the Body of Christ, we are one with Jesus and with one another.

■ We belong to the Catholic Church and to the Communion of Saints.

■ We work together as members of the Church.

Looking for More?

■ **www.FaithFirst.com**

■ **Faith First Legacy Edition** *Additional Activities* booklet for appropriate age level

■ **Faith First** videos (Grade 2—segment 6; Grade 5—segment 2; Junior High *Creed and Prayer*—segment 7; *Liturgy and Morality*—segment 2)

■ **Faith First Legacy Edition** *Called to Prayer* booklet for appropriate age level

■ Books to read, see pages 16 and 17

Family Blessing

God of all people,
bless us and be with us
as we learn how to live
as the People of God.
Amen.

PART 1

What We Already Know

Talk with your children to find out what they already know about the Church as the People of God. You can begin the discussion by using the example below or your own words.

We believe that the Church is the People of God. What do you think it means to be the People of God?

What We Will Discover

Provide time for the children to read and complete the activities.

Grade 1   Read pages 69–72 to discover how the saints help us.

Grade 2   Read pages 85–88 to discover how we live as members of the Church.

Grade 3   Read pages 69–72 to discover how the early Christians followed Jesus' example.

Grade 4   Read pages 85–88 to discover what the kingdom of God is.

Grade 5   Read pages 85–88 to discover what it means to live as members of the Church.

Grade 6   Read pages 69–72 to discover why the kingdom of God is so important to the teachings of Jesus.

Kindergarten Connection
Faith First Kindergarten Chapters 9 and 17
Junior High Connection
Faith First Legacy Edition Junior High *Church and Sacraments* Chapters 1 and 2

Sharing Together

You can use the following questions to discuss what the children have read. Be sure to answer any questions the children may have. Remember that the responses given below are simply one way to express the main idea underlying the response to each question, so be sure to affirm all appropriate responses.

■ *Who is the Church?*
(The Church is everyone who is baptized and believes in and follows Jesus. The Church is the People of God. The Church is the Body of Christ.)

■ *What do the members of the Church do?*
(Faithful members of the Church believe in Jesus and follow his teachings. We use our gifts to build up the Church.)

■ *Why do we call the Church the People of God?*
(Members of the Church belong to God. Through Baptism we are joined to Christ and become members of the Church.)

■ *In what ways is your family like the Church?*
(Responses will vary.)

■ *In what ways does your parish follow Jesus' example?*
(Responses will vary.)

All Grades Ask the children to share one or two things that they learned from their reading.

Working Together

Choose one of the following activities to do together or design a similar activity of your own.

■ List ways your parish follows Jesus' example. Use a parish bulletin as a reference to help you come up with your list.

■ List all of the people that take part in the celebration of Mass in your parish. Be sure to include the priest, music ministers, altar servers, greeters, ushers, readers, extraordinary ministers of Holy Communion, sacristans, liturgists, and everyone gathered. Notice that everyone has an important role in the celebration of Mass.

■ Research when and how your parish began. Find the answers to these and similar questions: Who were the first parishioners? Who was the first priest? How did the parishioners raise the money for the church to be built?

■ Make a poster explaining that the Church is the People of God. Write at the top of the poster "You can tell we are the People of God because . . ." Complete the statement, using drawings, words, and pictures from magazines or newspapers.

This week we will . . .

What Difference Does Faith Make?

Provide time for the children to read the "Our Church Makes a Difference" and the "What Difference Does Faith Make in My Life?" pages in their **Faith First Legacy Edition** books and complete the activities on those pages.

Grade 1 Read pages 73 and 74 and ask first graders to share one thing that they learned about the Church community. Have the children share their work and their faith choice on page 74.

Grade 2 Read pages 89 and 90 and ask second graders to share two things that they learned about Mary. Have the children share their work and their faith choice on page 90.

Grade 3 Read pages 73 and 74 and ask third graders to share two things that they learned about the Church. Have the children share their work and their faith choice on page 74.

Grade 4 Read pages 89 and 90 and ask fourth graders to share two things that they learned about the Communion of Saints. Have the children share their work and their faith decision on page 90.

Grade 5 Read pages 89 and 90 and ask fifth graders to share two things that they learned about devotion to Mary. Have the children share their work and their faith decision on page 90.

Grade 6 Read pages 73 and 74 and ask sixth graders to share two things that they learned about Saint Scholastica and Saint Benedict. Have the children share their work and their faith decision on page 74.

All Grades Discuss ways family members can help one another keep their faith choice or faith decision.

Kindergarten Connection
Ask the children to share what they learned this week.

Junior High Connection
Ask the children to share two things that they learned about the Church. Have the children share their faith decisions.

Praying Together

Ask each child to read and share the prayer page for this chapter of the child's book.

Have your family form a circle for prayer.

Light a candle and pray.

Leader: God of all people,
we are thankful for the time
we have shared today.
Be with us as we pray together.

Reader: (Read aloud 1 Corinthians 12:12–13.)

One at a time, ask each person to stand in the center of the circle. As each person stands in the circle, the other family members say together, "Lord, help _____ to use his (her) gifts for the good of the Church."

The person in the circle responds, "We are the People of God."

Conclude by praying the Apostles' Creed or the Nicene Creed together. Or sing these lyrics to the melody of "The Farmer in the Dell":
    The people are the Church.
    The people are the Church.
    Alleluia.
    The people are the Church.

Be sure to review the "With My Family" page in the child's book. "With My Family" is the last page of each chapter.

Baptism and Confirmation

Baptism is the first sacrament we celebrate and is closely related to Confirmation. Baptism is the entry door to life in the Church and is one of the three Sacraments of Christian Initiation. Through Baptism we are joined to Christ and become part of the Body of Christ, the Church.

At Baptism we make promises that we are to live out the rest of our lives. The Holy Spirit, whom we receive at Baptism, helps us live out the promises that we make. Confirmation completes the grace of Baptism by a special outpouring of the gifts of the Holy Spirit. The Holy Spirit is always with us as our companion and guide.

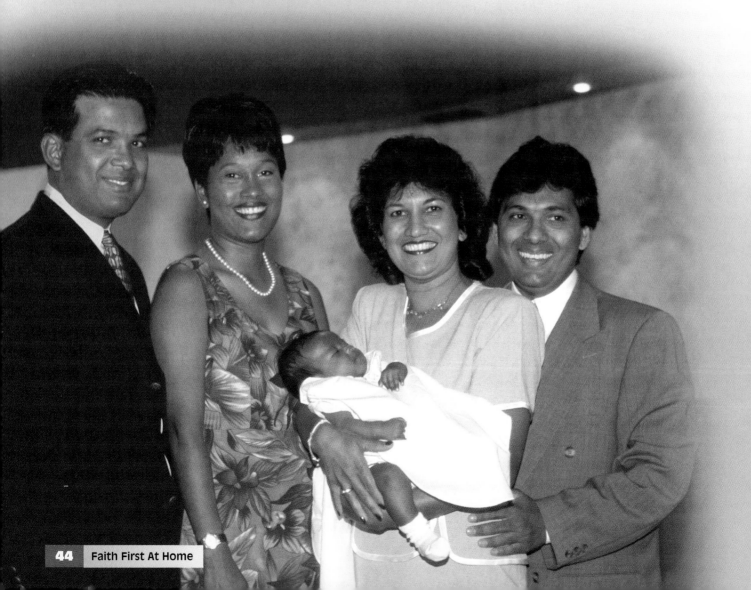

Using Our Faith First Legacy Edition Books

Use the following chapters to teach this lesson:

Grade 1 · Chapter 11
Grade 2 · Chapter 12
Grade 3 · Chapter 12
Grade 4 · Chapter 12
Grade 5 · Chapter 12
Grade 6 · Chapter 13

Kindergarten Connection
Faith First Kindergarten Chapter 15
Junior High Connection
Faith First Legacy Edition Junior High
Church and Sacraments Chapter 8

What We Will Learn

Through this lesson your family will learn that:

- Through the sacraments we share in the life and love of God.
- Through Baptism we become members of the Church and followers of Jesus Christ.
- In the celebration of Baptism we use specific words and actions.
- In the celebration of Confirmation we use specific words and actions.

Looking for More?

- **www.FaithFirst.com**
- **Faith First Legacy Edition** *Additional Activities* booklet for appropriate age level
- **Faith First** videos (Grade 5— segment 2; Junior High *Liturgy and Morality*—segment 7)
- **Faith First Legacy Edition** *Called to Prayer* booklet for appropriate age level
- Books to read, see pages 16 and 17

Family Blessing

God our Father and Creator,
through the waters of Baptism
we are joined to Christ, your Son.
Send the Holy Spirit to
be with us and bless us
as we learn to live as your children.
Amen.

PART 1

What We Already Know

Talk with your children to find out what they already know about Baptism and Confirmation. You can begin the discussion by using the example below or your own words.

In this lesson we are going to learn more about the sacraments of Baptism and Confirmation. What can you remember about Baptism and Confirmation? What happens at a celebration of Baptism? Who is there?

What We Will Discover

Provide time for the children to read and complete the activities.

Grade 1 Read pages 97–100 to discover why we celebrate Baptism.

Grade 2 Read pages 105–108 to discover the words and actions of Confirmation.

Grade 3 Read pages 105–108 to discover how the sacraments bring us closer to Jesus.

Grade 4 Read pages 105–108 to discover the names of all seven sacraments.

Grade 5 Read pages 105–108 to discover the effects of Baptism and Confirmation.

Grade 6 Read pages 113–116 to discover what the Church requires of those seeking Confirmation.

Kindergarten Connection
Faith First Kindergarten Chapter 15
Junior High Connection
Faith First Legacy Edition Junior High *Church and Sacraments* Chapter 8

Sharing Together

You can use the following questions to discuss what the children have read. Be sure to answer any questions the children may have. Remember that the responses given below are simply one way to express the main idea underlying the response to each question, so be sure to affirm all appropriate responses.

- *What do the sacraments celebrate?*
  (The sacraments celebrate God's love for us. The sacraments are celebrations of faith. Through the work of the Holy Spirit the sacraments make us sharers in the life of God and the work of Jesus Christ.)

- *Why do we celebrate Baptism?*
  (Through Baptism we are joined to Christ and become members of the Church. We receive the gift of the Holy Spirit. Original sin and our personal sins are forgiven. We are reborn as children of God.)

- *What are the words for Baptism?*
  ("I baptize you in the name of the Father, and of the Son, and of the Holy Spirit.")

- *What does the sacrament of Confirmation celebrate?*
  (Confirmation celebrates the Holy Spirit strengthening us to live as Christians.)

- *What are the words for Confirmation?*
  ("Be sealed with the Gift of the Holy Spirit.")

All Grades Ask the children to share one or two things that they learned from their reading.

Working Together

Choose one of the following activities to do together or design a similar activity of your own.

- Locate family photo albums, baby books, and other mementos from the Baptism of family members. Share stories about each person's Baptism. Be sure to tell why the day was so special for everyone present.

- Make cards for your godparents. Thank your godparents for helping you grow in a life of faith.

- Find videos your family may have of the Baptism and Confirmation of family members. Watch the videos and point out the words and actions of the sacraments.

- Make a calendar to help your family remember the days on which family members were baptized, confirmed, or celebrated First Eucharist. Decide how you will celebrate these special days.

This week we will . . .

What Difference Does Faith Make?

Provide time for the children to read the "Our Church Makes a Difference" and the "What Difference Does Faith Make in My Life?" pages in their **Faith First Legacy Edition** books and complete the activities on those pages.

Grade 1 Read pages 101 and 102 and ask first graders to share one thing that they learned about Project Star Fish. Have the children share their work and their faith choice on page 102.

Grade 2 Read pages 109 and 110 and ask second graders to share two things that they learned about Fiesta Grande. Have the children share their work and their faith choice on page 110.

Grade 3 Read pages 109 and 110 and ask third graders to share two things that they learned about sacramentals. Have the children share their work and their faith choice on page 110.

Grade 4 Read pages 109 and 110 and ask fourth graders to share two things that they learned about Bread for the World. Have the children share their work and their faith decision on page 110.

Grade 5 Read pages 109 and 110 and ask fifth graders to share two things that they learned about religious communities. Have the children share their work and their faith decision on page 110.

Grade 6 Read pages 117 and 118 and ask sixth graders to share two things that they learned about Saint Maximilian Kolbe. Have the children share their work and their faith decision on page 118.

All Grades Discuss ways family members can help one another keep their faith choice or faith decision.

Kindergarten Connection
Ask the children to share what they learned this week.

Junior High Connection
Ask the children to share two things that they learned about Baptism and Confirmation. Have the children share their faith decisions.

Praying Together

Ask each child to read and share the prayer page for this chapter of the child's book.

Put a small amount of water in a glass bowl. Then have your family form a circle for prayer.

Light a candle and pray.

Leader: Loving God,
we are thankful for the time
we have shared today.
Be with us as we pray together.

Pass the bowl of water from one person to another. As each person holds the bowl, the rest of the family says, "*(Name)*, be blessed by this water and remember the gift of your Baptism, in the name of the Father, and of the Son, and of the Holy Spirit."

The person with the bowl dips the fingers of their right hand into the water, makes the sign of the cross, and says aloud, "Amen."

Leader: God, Father of us all, at Baptism and Confirmation we celebrate the gift of the Holy Spirit. Help us remember to rely on the Holy Spirit so that we can live as your children. We ask this through Christ our Lord.

All: Amen.

Be sure to review the "With My Family" page in the child's book. "With My Family" is the last page of each chapter.

Eucharist and the Mass

The Second Vatican Council teaches that the Eucharist is the source and summit of the Christian life. In celebrating the Eucharist we share in the Paschal Mystery of the Passion, death, and Resurrection of Jesus Christ.

At Mass we celebrate both the Liturgy of the Word and the Liturgy of the Eucharist. These two parts of the Mass are closely linked. In listening to and reflecting on the Scriptures, we are fed by God's word. In remembering the Last Supper, in participating in Jesus' loving self-sacrifice, and in sharing Holy Communion and being nourished by the Body and Blood of Christ, we are joined more fully to Christ and to one another and strengthened to live the Gospel. God's power through the Holy Spirit makes Jesus truly present for us under the appearances of bread and wine. The bread and wine become the Body and Blood of Christ.

Celebrating the Eucharist each week with understanding and enthusiasm is an essential part of being Catholic. It is both a celebration of mystery and a source of unity among all Catholics.

Using Our Faith First Legacy Edition Books

Use the following chapters to teach this lesson:

Grade 1 · Chapter 13

Grade 2 · Chapter 15,
    see also chapters 16 and 17

Grade 3 · Chapter 13

Grade 4 · Chapter 12,
    see also chapter 13

Grade 5 · Chapter 14

Grade 6 · Chapter 15,
    see also chapter 12

Kindergarten Connection
Faith First Kindergarten Chapter 16
Junior High Connection
Faith First Legacy Edition Junior High
Church and Sacraments Chapters 6 and 9

What We Will Learn

Through this lesson your family will learn that:

- At Mass we praise and thank God.

- At Mass stories from the Bible are read during the Liturgy of the Word.

- We share the Body and Blood of Christ in the Eucharist.

- Our participation in Mass and our reverence for the Eucharist are at the heart of our life in Christ.

Looking for More?

- **www.FaithFirst.com**

- **Faith First Legacy Edition**
  Additional Activities booklet for appropriate age level

- **Faith First** videos (Gr. 2—segment 7; Gr. 3—segment 6; Gr. 5—segment 8; Gr. 6—segment 8; Junior High *Creed and Prayer*—segment 6; *Liturgy and Morality*—segment 6)

- **Faith First Legacy Edition** *Called to Prayer* booklet for appropriate age level

- Books to read, see pages 16 and 17

Family Blessing

Loving God,
be with our family
as we reflect upon
the great mystery of the
Eucharist.
Amen.

PART 1

What We Already Know

Talk with your children to find out what they already know about the Eucharist and the Mass. You can begin the discussion by using the example below or your own words.

As Catholics, we gather for Mass to celebrate the Eucharist. Let's share with one another some of the things that we see, hear, and do when we take part in the celebration of Mass.

What We Will Discover

Provide time for the children to read and complete the activities.

Grade 1 Read pages 113–116 to discover why we gather for Mass.

Grade 2 Read pages 129–132 to discover what we do during the Liturgy of the Word.

Grade 3 Read pages 113–116 to discover the meaning of the Blessed Sacrament.

Grade 4 Read pages 105–108 to discover the ways that Jesus is present with us in every celebration of the Eucharist.

Grade 5 Read pages 121–124 to discover how we celebrate the Mass.

Grade 6 Read pages 129–132 to discover how the Old Testament helps us understand the meaning of the Eucharist.

Kindergarten Connection
Faith First Kindergarten Chapter 16
Junior High Connection
Faith First Legacy Edition Junior High *Church and Sacraments* Chapters 6 and 9

Sharing Together

You can use the following questions to discuss what the children have read. Be sure to answer any questions the children may have. Remember that the responses given below are simply one way to express the main idea underlying the response to each question, so be sure to affirm all appropriate responses.

■ *Why do we gather for Mass?*
(We gather as the Church community for the celebration of Mass to listen to God's word and to praise and thank God.)

■ *What do we do during the Liturgy of the Word?*
(During the Liturgy of the Word, we listen to stories from the Bible: usually an Old Testament reading, a psalm, a New Testament reading, and a Gospel reading.)

■ *What happens during the Liturgy of the Eucharist?*
(We share in the Paschal Mystery of Christ, his Passion, death, Resurrection, and Ascension. The bread and wine become the Body and Blood of Christ. We receive the Body and Blood of Christ in Holy Communion.)

■ *How do we participate in the celebration of Mass?*
(We participate in Mass when we sing and say the responses. We stand or kneel. We pray. Joined to Christ, we offer ourselves to God. We share a sign of peace. We receive the Eucharist.)

All Grades Ask the children to share one or two things that they learned from their reading.

Working Together

Choose one of the following activities to do together or design a similar activity of your own.

■ Saint Pius X had a special devotion to the Eucharist. Search your parish library, a public library, or the Internet to see if you can find out more about Saint Pius X.

■ Before you take part in the celebration of Mass next weekend, together read the Gospel selection assigned for that Sunday. Talk about what this reading means for your family.

■ Go together to see the tabernacle at your church. Explain that we believe that Christ is present in the Eucharist. We call the consecrated bread, or the Eucharist, the Blessed Sacrament. We keep, or reserve, the Blessed Sacrament in a tabernacle to show our reverence and respect for the Eucharist and to be able to bring Holy Communion to those who are ill or elderly and cannot get to church for the celebration of Mass. Notice the lit candle near the tabernacle. It is called a sanctuary lamp. It tells us that the Blessed Sacrament is in the tabernacle.

■ See how many of the liturgical ministers at Mass you can list. Your list might include priest, altar servers, readers or lectors, extraordinary ministers of Holy Communion, greeters, ushers, sacristan, musicians, singers, and so on. Your parish might even have a liturgy planning team, a group that prepares the environment or a volunteer cleaning crew.

This week we will . . .

_____

_____

_____

_____

_____

_____

What Difference Does Faith Make?

Provide time for the children to read the "Our Church Makes a Difference" and the "What Difference Does Faith Make in My Life?" pages in their **Faith First Legacy Edition** books and complete the activities on those pages.

Grade 1 Read pages 117 and 118 and ask first graders to share one thing they learned about how the Mass helps us live as disciples. Have the children share their work and their faith choice on page 118.

Grade 2 Read pages 133 and 134 and ask second graders to share two things that they learned about processions. Have the children share their work and their faith choice on page 134.

Grade 3 Read pages 117 and 118 and ask third graders to share two things that they learned about the holy days of obligation. Have the children share their work and their faith choice on page 118.

Grade 4 Read pages 109 and 110 and ask fourth graders to share two things that they learned about Bread for the World. Have the children share their work and their faith decision on page 110.

Grade 5 Read pages 125 and 126 and ask fifth graders to share two things that they learned about Blessed Teresa of Calcutta. Have the children share their work and their faith decision on page 126.

Grade 6 Read pages 133 and 134 and ask sixth graders to share two things that they learned about Archbishop Oscar Romero. Have the children share their work and their faith decision on page 134.

All Grades Discuss ways family members can help one another keep their faith choice or faith decision.

Kindergarten Connection
Ask the children to share what they learned this week.
Junior High Connection
Ask the children to share two things that they learned about Bread for the World. Have the children share their faith decisions.

Praying Together

Ask each child to read and share the prayer page for this chapter of the child's book.

Give everyone a few minutes to write petitions for a prayer similar to the petitions that are part of the Prayer of the Faithful we pray at Mass. Remind everyone to conclude their petitions, "We pray to the Lord." You might have older children help younger children. Then gather the group for prayer.

Light a candle and pray.

Leader: God our Creator,
we are thankful for the time
we have shared today.
Be with us as we pray together.

Reader: (Read aloud the story of the Last Supper, Matthew 26:26–30.)

Ask each person to pray their petitions aloud. After each person prays aloud, the rest of the family responds, "Lord, hear our prayer."

Leader: As a sign of our unity as Catholics, let us pray as Jesus taught us.

All: Our Father . . .

Be sure to review the "With My Family" page in the child's book. "With My Family" is the last page of each chapter.

Reconciliation and Anointing of the Sick

When Jesus walked among us, he forgave sins and restored the health of numerous people whom he met. This healing now stretches out through the Church, the Body of Christ, to all who call upon Jesus for help. Through the sacrament of Reconciliation we receive forgiveness for the sins we have committed after we have been baptized when we are truly sorry for our sins, confess them to a priest, receive and do a penance, and are absolved from our sins. The healing forgiveness of God restores us to spiritual health. We become renewed members of the Body of Christ.

Through the sacrament of Anointing of the Sick we also share in the healing ministry of Jesus. This sacrament brings Christ's compassion to our deepest needs in times of serious illness or old age. Christ inspires us with hope and courage and gives us the promise of salvation. We respond in faith, turn our fear over to Christ, and trust in God's love and healing presence with us.

Using Our Faith First Legacy Edition Books

Use the following chapters to teach this lesson:

Grade 1 · Chapter 11, pages 98 and 99

Grade 2 · Chapter 14

Grade 3 · Chapter 15

Grade 4 · Chapter 14

Grade 5 · Chapter 16

Grade 6 · Chapter 17

Kindergarten Connection
Faith First Kindergarten Chapter 23
Junior High Connection
Faith First Legacy Edition Junior High
Church and Sacraments Chapter 11

What We Will Learn

Through this lesson your family will learn that:

- We prepare for the sacrament of Reconciliation by thinking about the choices we have made.

- We receive absolution for our sins in the sacrament of Reconciliation.

- The sacrament of Anointing of the Sick strengthens us and encourages us in times of serious illness or old age.

- The Church continues Jesus' healing ministry in the world.

Looking for More?

- **www.FaithFirst.com**

- **Faith First Legacy Edition** *Additional Activities* booklet for appropriate age level

- **Faith First** videos (Grade 4— segment 2; Junior High *Liturgy and Morality*—segments 3, 4)

- **Faith First Legacy Edition** *Called to Prayer* booklet for appropriate age level

- Books to read, see pages 16 and 17

Family Blessing

Loving God,
Creator of our immense universe,
be with us and bless us
as we reflect upon your loving-kindness,
which we receive
through the Sacraments of Healing.
Amen.

PART 1

What We Already Know

Talk with your children to find out what they already know about the Sacraments of Healing: Reconciliation and Anointing of the Sick. You can begin the discussion by using the example below or your own words.

Share any experiences you have of the Sacraments of Healing.
What are some of the actions and the words of these sacraments?
Why are Reconciliation and Anointing of the Sick called Sacraments of Healing?

What We Will Discover

Provide time for the children to read and complete the activities.

Grade 1   Read pages 98–99 to discover the names of all seven sacraments.

Grade 2   Read pages 121–124 to discover what happens when we celebrate the sacrament of Reconciliation.

Grade 3   Read pages 129–132 to discover why we celebrate the sacrament of Anointing of the Sick.

Grade 4   Read pages 121–124 to discover why we describe Jesus' work among us as the work of healing and forgiveness.

Grade 5   Read pages 137–140 to discover the parts of the sacrament of Reconciliation.

Grade 6   Read pages 145–148 to discover the spiritual effects of the sacrament of Reconciliation.

Kindergarten Connection
Faith First Kindergarten Chapter 23
Junior High Connection
Faith First Legacy Edition Junior High *Church and Sacraments* Chapter 11

Sharing Together

You can use the following questions to discuss what the children have read. Be sure to answer any questions the children may have. Remember that the responses given below are simply one way to express the main idea underlying the response to each question, so be sure to affirm all appropriate responses.

- *Why do we celebrate the sacrament of Reconciliation?*
(We celebrate the sacrament of Reconciliation to ask for and receive God's forgiveness for our sins.)

- *What are the four parts of the sacrament of Reconciliation?*
(The four parts of Reconciliation are being truly sorry for our sins, or contrition; confessing our sins to a priest; receiving and doing a penance; and receiving absolution.)

- *Why do we celebrate the sacrament of Anointing of the Sick?*
(We celebrate the sacrament of Anointing of the Sick to receive strength, courage, and peace in times of serious illness or old age. This sacrament can help prepare people for death and the journey into heaven.)

- *How does your parish continue the healing ministry of Jesus?*
(Responses might include: Our parish visits people who are in hospitals, who are homebound, and who are in nursing homes.)

All Grades Ask the children to share one or two things that they learned from their reading.

Working Together

Choose one of the following activities to do together or design a similar activity of your own.

- The story of Zacchaeus is one of many stories about forgiveness in the Bible. Read together Luke 19:1–10 and discuss ways that people might seek forgiveness.

- To help your children better understand the sacrament of Reconciliation, pantomime the steps of the sacrament with them. Be sure to include thinking about our choices and praying an act of contrition, confessing our sins, receiving a penance, and receiving absolution.

- Talk about the importance of forgiveness in your family. Retell a family story about forgiveness.

- Call your parish office and find out when the sacrament of Anointing of the Sick is celebrated during the celebration of Mass. Plan for your whole family to participate in the celebration.

- Many of the saints are wonderful examples of people who ministered to the sick. Search your parish library, public library, or the Internet for information on one of these saints: Saint Elizabeth Ann Seton, Saint Frances Cabrini, Saint Elizabeth of Hungary, Saint Jude. Gather and share interesting points regarding the lives of one or more of these saints.

This week we will . . .

_____

_____

_____

_____

_____

_____

_____

What Difference Does Faith Make?

Provide time for the children to read the "Our Church Makes a Difference" and the "What Difference Does Faith Make in My Life?" pages in their **Faith First Legacy Edition** books and complete the activities on those pages.

Grade 1 Read pages 101 and 102 and ask first graders to share one thing they learned about Operation Rice Bowl. Have the children share their work and their faith choice on page 102.

Grade 2 Read pages 125 and 126 and ask second graders to share two things that they learned about Saint Dominic Savio. Have the children share their work and their faith choice on page 126.

Grade 3 Read pages 133 and 134 and ask third graders to share two things that they learned about Pope John Paul II and forgiveness. Have the children share their work and their faith choice on page 134.

Grade 4 Read pages 125 and 126 and ask fourth graders to share two things that they learned about parish ministers to the sick. Have the children share their work and their faith decision on page 126.

Grade 5 Read pages 141 and 142 and ask fifth graders to share two things that they learned about Catholic hospitals. Have the children share their work and their faith decision on page 142.

Grade 6 Read pages 149 and 150 and ask sixth graders to share two things that they learned about hospice. Have the children share their work and their faith decision on page 150.

All Grades Discuss ways family members can help one another keep their faith choice or faith decision.

Kindergarten Connection
Ask the children to share what they learned this week.

Junior High Connection
Ask the children to share two things that they learned about the Sacraments of Healing. Have the children share their faith decisions.

Praying Together

Ask each child to read and share the prayer page for this chapter of the child's book.

Give everyone a minute or two to find an object in your home that symbolizes forgiveness or healing. Then have the group form a circle for prayer.

Light a candle and pray.

Leader: God our Creator,
we are thankful for the time
we have shared today.
Be with us as we pray together.

Reader: (Read aloud Matthew 9:23–26.)

One at a time, invite each person to bring the object to the center of the group. As each person does this, the rest of the group says together:
(Name), may God the Father bless you.
May God the Son heal you.
May God the Holy Spirit enlighten you.
(From *Pastoral Care of the Sick*)

Leader: God our Father, help us remember always to continue Christ's healing ministry. Send the Holy Spirit to give us the strength to be willing to ask for forgiveness as well as to forgive one another. We ask this through Christ our Lord.

All: Amen.

Be sure to review the "With My Family" page in the child's book. "With My Family" is the last page of each chapter.

Holy Orders and Matrimony

Holy Orders and Matrimony, the two Sacraments at the Service of Communion, consecrate, or set apart, members of the Body of Christ for service to the entire Church community. Through the sacrament of Holy Orders, priests and bishops share in the priesthood of Christ in a unique way so that they can act in the name and person of Jesus Christ, Head and Shepherd, for the sake of the whole Church. Deacons are ordained to help priests and bishops in this mission. Bishops, priests, and deacons serve the Church by proclaiming and preaching God's word, leading us in celebrating the sacraments, and guiding us in living the Gospel.

In the sacrament of Matrimony a baptized woman and a baptized man are joined in marriage for life and are called to serve the whole Church together as a married couple. A couple joined in Matrimony establishes a domestic church, which means a church in their household. The family itself is a sign to the world of God's everlasting love for all people. The love and support of a husband and a wife for each other is a sign of God's ongoing loving care for all people and of Christ's love for the Church.

Using Our Faith First Legacy Edition Books

Use the following chapters to teach this lesson:

Grade 1 · Chapter 12

Grade 2 · Chapter 11, pages 100-101

Grade 3 · Chapter 17

Grade 4 · Chapter 16

Grade 5 · Chapter 17

Grade 6 · Chapter 18

Kindergarten Connection
Faith First Kindergarten Chapter 8
Junior High Connection
Faith First Legacy Edition Junior High
Church and Sacraments Chapter 12

What We Will Learn

Through this lesson your family will learn that:

■ We are all called to holiness.

■ Jesus teaches us to follow his example and serve others.

■ Through the sacrament of Holy Orders, bishops, priests, and deacons are called to serve the whole Church.

■ Through the sacrament of Matrimony God calls a baptized man and a baptized woman to serve the Church as a married couple.

Looking for More?

■ **www.FaithFirst.com**

■ **Faith First Legacy Edition** *Additional Activities* booklet for appropriate age level

■ **Faith First** videos (Grade 2— segment 6; Junior High *Liturgy and Morality*—segment 3)

■ **Faith First Legacy Edition** *Called to Prayer* booklet for appropriate age level

■ Books to read, see pages 16 and 17

Family Blessing

*Loving God,
be with us and bless us
as we come to understand
that each of us
is called to holiness.
Amen.*

PART 1

What We Already Know

Talk with your children to find out what they already know about the sacraments of Holy Orders and Matrimony. You can begin the discussion by using the example below or your own words.

Share any experiences you have of ordinations or weddings. What are some of the words or actions that you can recall from the celebration of the sacrament of Holy Orders and the sacrament of Matrimony?

What We Will Discover

Provide time for the children to read and complete the activities.

Grade 1   Read pages 105–108 to discover what Jesus told his followers to do.

Grade 2   Read pages 100 and 101 to discover the names of all seven sacraments.

Grade 3   Read pages 145–148 to discover our vocation as Christians.

Grade 4   Read pages 137–140 to discover why the Church celebrates the sacrament of Holy Orders.

Grade 5   Read pages 145–148 to discover why the Church celebrates the sacrament of Matrimony.

Grade 6   Read pages 153–156 to discover what the Church means by the terms *service* and *communion*.

Kindergarten Connection
Faith First Kindergarten Chapter 8
Junior High Connection
Faith First Legacy Edition Junior High *Church and Sacraments* Chapter 12

Sharing Together

You can use the following questions to discuss what the children have read. Be sure to answer any questions the children may have. Remember that the responses given below are simply one way to express the main idea underlying the response to each question, so be sure to affirm all appropriate responses.

- *How do deacons serve the Church?*
  (Deacons help bishops and priests. They proclaim the Gospel at Mass. They also baptize, marry people, and bury the dead. They often minister to the sick and people in need.)

- *How do priests serve the Church?*
  (Priests are coworkers with their bishop. They preach the Gospel and preside over the Eucharist and other sacraments. They lead parishes and serve the Church in many other ways.)

- *How do bishops serve the Church?*
  (Bishops are successors of the Apostles. They are responsible for preaching the Gospel, teaching the faith, presiding over all the sacraments, and guiding us in living as faithful followers of Christ.)

- *How do Christian married couples serve the Church?*
  (Married couples love, care for, honor, and respect each other. Christian married couples raise their children to live as followers of Christ. They are signs of Jesus' love for the Church. They help us learn how we can show our love for God and other people.)

All Grades Ask the children to share one or two things that they learned from their reading.

Working Together

Choose one of the following activities to do together or design a similar activity of your own.

- How does your family live as followers of Jesus? Talk about the many ways that members of your family help and serve one another. Discuss how your family is holy. For example, share ways that you encourage one another, trust one another, or celebrate important days together.

- Make and send thank-you notes to a bishop, priest, deacon, or married couple. Thank them for their service to the Church. Be sure to share with them how their service has made a difference in the life of your family.

- Find pictures from a family wedding. Share memories of the wedding. Identify and talk about the words and actions that are part of the celebration of the sacrament of Matrimony.

- Look at your parish bulletin to discover the many ways the people in your parish are serving others. Try to think of a few more ways people in your parish can serve others.

This week we will . . .

What Difference Does Faith Make?

Provide time for the children to read the "Our Church Makes a Difference" and the "What Difference Does Faith Make in My Life?" pages in their **Faith First Legacy Edition** books and complete the activities on those pages.

Grade 1 Read pages 109 and 110 and ask first graders to share one thing they learned about Saint Francis of Assisi. Have the children share their work and their faith choice on page 110.

Grade 2 Read pages 101 and 102 and ask second graders to share two things that they learned about sacrament words and actions. Have the children share their work and their faith choice on page 102.

Grade 3 Read pages 149 and 150 and ask third graders to share two things that they learned about Catholic Relief Services. Have the children share their work and their faith choice on page 150.

Grade 4 Read pages 141 and 142 and ask fourth graders to share two things that they learned about religious brothers and sisters. Have the children share their work and their faith decision on page 142.

Grade 5 Read pages 149 and 150 and ask fifth graders to share two things that they learned about working together in a parish. Have the children share their work and their faith decision on page 150.

Grade 6 Read pages 157 and 158 and ask sixth graders to share two things that they learned about the domestic church. Have the children share their work and their faith decision on page 158.

All Grades Discuss ways family members can help one another keep their faith choice or faith decision.

Kindergarten Connection
Ask the children to share what they learned this week.

Junior High Connection
Ask the children to share two things that they learned about Holy Orders and Matrimony. Have the children share their faith decisions.

Praying Together

Ask each child to read and share the prayer page for this chapter of the child's book.

Find a candle that you can safely pass to each family member during prayer. Gather the group for prayer.

Light a candle and pray.

Leader: God our Creator,
we are thankful for the time
we have shared today.
Be with us as we pray together.

Reader: (Read aloud John 13:1–17, the story of Jesus washing the disciples' feet.)

Pass the candle around the group from one person to another. As each person holds the candle, the group says, "*(Name)*, may you always live a life of service just as Jesus did."

The person holding the candle responds, "Amen."

Leader: God, help us remember that you call each of us to holiness. Guide us and encourage us to serve one another. We ask this through Christ our Lord.

All: Amen.

Be sure to review the "With My Family" page in the child's book. "With My Family" is the last page of each chapter.

The Church's Year of Worship

The Church's liturgical year is an annual cycle of seasons and feasts that celebrate Christ's birth, life, Passion, death, Resurrection, and Ascension. Foremost among these celebrations is Easter—the celebration of Christ's Resurrection.

The liturgical year begins each year with Advent. During this liturgical season we prepare to remember Christ's birth at Christmas as the Savior of the world and his Second Coming at the end of time. The celebration of the Christmas season begins in the evening of Christmas Eve and continues until the Sunday after the Epiphany, which is the feast of the Baptism of the Lord.

The Church next celebrates several weeks of Ordinary Time until Ash Wednesday, which marks the beginning of Lent. During Lent we prepare for Easter. Lent is a time to prepare to

welcome new members into the Church and for the faithful to renew their own baptismal promises. Lent concludes on Holy Thursday with the celebration of the Evening Mass of the Lord's Supper, which begins the Easter Triduum. The Easter Triduum is the center of the liturgical year. The fifty days of the Easter season are celebrated as one feast, or "great Sunday," of joy.

All the remaining weeks, which number about thirty-three weeks, are known as Ordinary Time. During this time we reflect on the life and ministry of Jesus and strive to live as his faithful followers.

Using Our Faith First Legacy Edition Books

Use the following chapters to teach this lesson:

Grade 1 · Chapter 10

Grade 2 · The Liturgical Year/Ordinary Time

Grade 3 · Chapter 11

Grade 4 · Chapter 11

Grade 5 · Chapter 11

Grade 6 · Chapter 11

Kindergarten Connection
Have your child work with another child for this lesson.

Junior High Connection
Have your child work with another child for this lesson.

What We Will Learn

Through this lesson your family will learn that:

■ The Church divides the year into liturgical seasons.

■ The seasons of the Church's year are Advent, Christmas, Lent, Easter, and Ordinary Time.

■ The center of the liturgical year is the Easter Triduum, when we remember that Jesus died and was raised to new life.

Looking for More?

■ **www.FaithFirst.com**

■ **Faith First Legacy Edition** *Additional Activities* booklet for appropriate age level

■ **Faith First Legacy Edition** *Called to Prayer* booklet for appropriate age level

■ Books to read, see pages 16 and 17

Family Blessing

Loving God,
be with us and bless us
as we come to appreciate more fully
the liturgical seasons of the Church.
Amen.

PART 1

What We Already Know

Talk with your children to find out what they already know about the seasons of the Church's year. You can begin the discussion by using the example below or your own words.

The Church divides the year into liturgical seasons. What liturgical seasons can you name? What is your favorite liturgical season and why?

What We Will Discover

Provide time for the children to read and complete the activities.

Grade 1   Read pages 89–92 to discover what the Church celebrates during Advent and Christmas.

Grade 2   Read pages 237 and 238 to discover how the Church celebrates our faith throughout the year.

Grade 3   Read pages 97–100 to discover when the Church most fully celebrates the Paschal Mystery.

Grade 4   Read pages 97–100 to discover how the Church celebrates the good news of God's love for us all year.

Grade 5   Read pages 97–100 to discover how the Church celebrates the liturgical year.

Grade 6   Read pages 97–100 to discover how the Church celebrates the liturgical year.

Kindergarten Connection
Have your child work with another child for this lesson.

Junior High Connection
Have your child work with another child for this lesson.

PART 2

Sharing Together

You can use the following questions to discuss what the children have read. Be sure to answer any questions the children may have. Remember that the responses given below are simply one way to express the main idea underlying the response to each question, so be sure to affirm all appropriate responses.

■ *What do we call the Church's year?*
(The Church's year is called the liturgical year.)

■ *What are the seasons of the Church's year?*
(The seasons of the liturgical year of the Church are Advent, Christmas, Lent, Easter, and Ordinary Time. The Easter Triduum is the center of the liturgical year.)

■ *What do we celebrate during Advent and Christmas?*
(During Advent we prepare to celebrate Jesus' birth at Christmas and his Second Coming at the end of time. During Christmas we celebrate Jesus' birth as the Savior of the world.)

■ *What do we celebrate during Lent and Easter?*
(Lent is a time to remember that Jesus died for us. We get ready for Easter. We prepare and welcome new members into the Church. We celebrate Jesus' Resurrection during Easter.)

■ *What kinds of stories do we hear about Jesus at Mass during Ordinary Time?*
(We hear stories of Jesus teaching, healing, and performing miracles.)

All Grades Ask the children to share one or two things that they learned from their reading.

Working Together

Choose one of the following activities to do together or design a similar activity of your own.

■ Identify and talk about the sights, smells, and sounds of both the seasons of the liturgical year and of the seasons of the calendar year.

■ Invite the children to draw pictures of ways that they celebrate one of the Church's seasons. Have each child share the drawing with everyone.

■ Find out what liturgical season the Church is celebrating right now. Make place mats for your table that will help you celebrate and remember the liturgical season. You might even make a set of place mats to use for each liturgical season.

■ The next time your family takes part in the celebration of Mass, notice the liturgical colors of the environment and vestments. Talk about what liturgical season the Church is celebrating. You might like to add the appropriate liturgical colors to a place in your home where your family gathers for prayer.

This week we will . . .

_____

_____

_____

_____

_____

_____

_____

_____

_____

What Difference Does Faith Make?

Provide time for the children to read the "Our Church Makes a Difference" and the "What Difference Does Faith Make in My Life?" pages in their **Faith First Legacy Edition** books and complete the activities on those pages.

Grade 1 Read pages 93 and 94 and ask first graders to share one thing they learned about the Lord's Day. Have the children share their work and their faith choice on page 94.

Grade 2 There are no "What Difference" pages for the liturgical seasons section of the child's book. Have your second grader share a book with another child.

Grade 3 Read pages 101 and 102 and ask third graders to share two things that they learned about Church feasts of the Lord. Have the children share their work and their faith choice on page 102.

Grade 4 Read pages 101 and 102 and ask fourth graders to share two things that they learned about Las Posadas. Have the children share their work and their faith decision on page 102.

Grade 5 Read pages 101 and 102 and ask fifth graders to share two things that they learned about Church feasts of the Lord. Have the children share their work and their faith decision on page 102.

Grade 6 Read pages 101 and 102 and ask sixth graders to share two things that they learned about the celebration of the sacraments. Have the children share their work and their faith decision on page 102.

All Grades Discuss ways family members can help one another keep their faith choice or faith decision.

Kindergarten Connection
Ask the children to share what they learned this week.

Junior High Connection
Ask the children to share two things that they learned about the liturgical seasons of the Church's year. Have the children share their faith decisions.

Praying Together

Ask each child to read and share the prayer page for this chapter of the child's book.

Give everyone a minute or two to find an object that is the color of their favorite liturgical season. Then gather the group for prayer.

Light a candle and pray.

Leader: Living God,
we are thankful for the time
we have shared today.
Be with us as we pray together.

Invite each person to come forward with the object that they have chosen. As each person comes forward, the rest of the group says, "*(Name)*, may you grow in faith as you celebrate with the Church."

The person responds, "Amen."

Leader: God, you are always with us. Remind us to give you praise every day and celebrate your presence throughout the year. We ask this through Christ our Lord.

All: Amen.

Be sure to review the "With My Family" page in the child's book. "With My Family" is the last page of each chapter.

Loving God

Each day we make choices to live as children of God and followers of Christ. The Ten Commandments guide us in making those choices. The first three Commandments focus on our relationship with God. The First Commandment is "I am the LORD your God: you shall not have strange Gods before me." This Commandment teaches that we have been created by and for God. God is our beginning and our end. We have been created to live in communion with God. No one and nothing else comes before God.

The Second Commandment is "You shall not take the name of the LORD your God in vain." This Commandment demands respect for God. The Second Commandment concerns not swearing or saying the names of God, Jesus, Mary, or those of the saints in an offensive way.

The Third Commandment is "Remember to keep holy the LORD's Day." This Commandment requires us to set time aside to focus on God—to worship, to give thanks, and to enjoy God who loves us and is the source of our life and happiness. For Catholics this means participating in the Eucharist every Sunday.

Using Our Faith First Legacy Edition Books

Use the following chapters to teach this lesson:

Kindergarten Connection
Faith First Kindergarten Chapter 20
Junior High Connection
Faith First Legacy Edition Junior High
Morality: Life in Christ Chapter 7

What We Will Learn

Through this lesson your family will learn that:

- The Ten Commandments are laws revealed by God.
- The first three Commandments help us love God.
- Jesus taught us to live as children of God.

Looking for More?

- www.FaithFirst.com
- **Faith First Legacy Edition** *Additional Activities* booklet for appropriate age level
- **Faith First** videos (Grade 2— segment 3; Grade 4—segment 4)
- **Faith First Legacy Edition** *Called to Prayer* booklet for appropriate age level
- Books to read, see pages 16 and 17

Family Blessing

Loving God,
be with us and bless us
as we learn to live
your Commandments
in gratitude and trust.
Amen.

PART 1

What We Already Know

Talk with your children to find out what they already know about loving God. You can begin the discussion by using the example below or your own words.

The first three Commandments teach us to love God. Let's share with one another some of the ways we show our love for God.

What We Will Discover

Provide time for the children to read and complete the activities.

Grade 1   Read pages 165–168 to discover ways that we can show our love for God.

Grade 2   Read pages 157–160 to discover ways that we show we are children of God.

Grade 3   Read pages 165–168 to discover why the Ten Commandments are important.

Grade 4   Read pages 181–184 to discover how the Third Commandment helps us worship God.

Grade 5   Read pages 189–192 to discover how the First and Second Commandments help us live as children of God.

Grade 6   Read pages 181–184 to discover what the first three Commandments teach us about ourselves.

Kindergarten Connection
Faith First Kindergarten Chapter 20
Junior High Connection
Faith First Legacy Edition Junior High *Morality: Life in Christ* Chapter 7

Sharing Together

You can use the following questions to discuss what the children have read. Be sure to answer any questions the children may have. Remember that the responses given below are simply one way to express the main idea underlying the response to each question, so be sure to affirm all appropriate responses.

■ *What are the Ten Commandments?*
(The Ten Commandments are the laws revealed by God to Moses and the Israelites on Mount Sinai. The Ten Commandments tell us ways that we are to love God, others, and ourselves.)

■ *Why are the Ten Commandments important?*
(The Ten Commandments help us show our love for God, other people, and ourselves.)

■ *How can we show our love for God?*
(We show our love for God when we keep him first in our lives, when we speak God's name with honor and respect, and when we keep Sunday holy and worship God.)

All Grades Ask the children to share one or two things that they learned from their reading.

Working Together

Choose one of the following activities to do together or design a similar activity of your own.

■ Discuss these or similar questions as a family to help the children appreciate how rules and laws help us: What if you only went to school when you wanted to? What if your family let you only eat the foods you liked? What if there were no traffic signals or stop signs in our community?

■ The Third Commandment reminds us to keep Sundays holy. Together plan several ways you can make next Sunday a special and holy day for your family.

■ Using clay, have the children make their own Ten Commandment tablets. The children can etch the numerals 1 to 10 into the clay. When the tablets dry, they will serve as reminders to live the Ten Commandments.

■ Together rewrite the first three Commandments in language the children can understand. Replace the words "you shall" with the words "we will."

This week we will . . .

_____

_____

_____

_____

_____

_____

_____

_____

_____

What Difference Does Faith Make?

Provide time for the children to read the "Our Church Makes a Difference" and the "What Difference Does Faith Make in My Life?" pages in their **Faith First Legacy Edition** books and complete the activities on those pages.

Grade 1 Read pages 169 and 170 and ask first graders to share one thing they learned about the Poor Clares. Have the children share their work and their faith choice on page 170.

Grade 2 Read pages 161 and 162 and ask second graders to share two things that they learned about Saint Thérèse of Lisieux. Have the children share their work and their faith choice on page 162.

Grade 3 Read pages 169 and 170 and ask third graders to share two things that they learned about churches. Have the children share their work and their faith choice on page 170.

Grade 4 Read pages 185 and 186 and ask fourth graders to share two things that they learned about Saint Joan of Arc. Have the children share their work and their faith decision on page 186.

Grade 5 Read pages 193 and 194 and ask fifth graders to share two things that they learned about holy days. Have the children share their work and their faith decision on page 194.

Grade 6 Read pages 185 and 186 and ask sixth graders to share two things that they learned about the collection at Mass. Have the children share their work and their faith decision on page 186.

All Grades Discuss ways family members can help one another keep their faith choice or faith decision.

Kindergarten Connection

Ask the children to share what they learned this week.

Junior High Connection

Ask the children to share two things that they learned about loving God. Have the children share their faith decisions.

Praying Together

Ask each child to read and share the prayer page for this chapter of the child's book.

Write each of the first three Commandments on a slip of paper and distribute the papers among family members. Then gather your family for prayer.

Light a candle and pray.

Leader: Living God,
we are thankful for the time
we have shared today.
Be with us as we pray together.

Reader: (Read aloud Psalm 119:33–34.)

One at a time, ask family members to read aloud the Commandment that is written on the paper you have given them. After each Commandment is read aloud, the rest of the family responds, "We will live God's Commandments."

Leader: God, help us remember always to live by your Commandments and to show our love for you. We ask this through Christ our Lord.

All: Amen.

Be sure to review the "With My Family" page in the child's book. "With My Family" is the last page of each chapter.

Loving Others

The last seven of the Ten Commandments teach us how to love and respect our neighbors, ourselves, and creation. We are to respect our families, human life, sexuality, the fruit of human labor, truth, purity, and ourselves.

The Fourth Commandment directs us to honor our parents, to whom we owe our lives, and others who exercise authority legitimately in society. The Fifth Commandment teaches that all life is sacred and commands us to respect all human life. The Sixth Commandment teaches us to respect and honor our sexuality and to share our love with one another in appropriate ways, following Christ as our model.

The Seventh Commandment helps us live out justice and charity in our relationships with other people. The Eighth Commandment directs us to respect truth so that we do not misrepresent it in our relations with others. The Ninth Commandment calls us to be pure in mind and heart, as well as in our actions. The Tenth Commandment counsels us to respect our possessions and the possessions of others as blessings from God and to share our blessings with others.

Using Our Faith First Legacy Edition Books

Use the following chapters to teach this lesson:

Kindergarten Connection
Faith First Kindergarten Chapter 21
Junior High Connection
Faith First Legacy Edition Junior High *Morality: Life in Christ* Chapters 9 and 10 and *Jesus in the New Testament* Chapter 9

What We Will Learn

Through this lesson your family will learn that:

■ The Fourth Commandment teaches us to honor and respect our parents.

■ The Fifth through Tenth Commandments teach us how to love and treat people respectfully, to care for life, to be faithful, to respect others, and to be truthful and generous.

Looking for More?

■ **www.FaithFirst.com**

■ **Faith First Legacy Edition** *Additional Activities* booklet for appropriate age level

■ **Faith First** videos (Gr. 1—segment 5; Gr. 3—segment 4; Gr. 4—segment 4; Gr. 5—segment 5; Gr. 6—segments 4 and 6; Junior High *Creed and Prayer*—segment 5; *Liturgy and Morality*— segment 5)

■ **Faith First Legacy Edition** *Called to Prayer* booklet for appropriate age level

■ Books to read, see pages 16 and 17

Family Blessing

Loving God,
be with us and bless us
as we learn how to live
the spirit of your laws,
which you generously
revealed to us.
Amen.

PART 1

What We Already Know

Talk with your children to find out what they already know about loving others. You can begin the discussion by using the example below or your own words.

The Fourth through Tenth Commandments teach us to respect and love others. Let's share with one another some ways that we can show love and respect for others as Jesus taught us.

What We Will Discover

Provide time for the children to read and complete the activities.

Grade 1   Read pages 173–176 to discover what the Ten Commandments teach us about respect.

Grade 2   Read pages 173–176 to discover ways that we show respect for the property of others.

Grade 3   Read pages 173–176 to discover ways we can keep the Fourth Commandment.

Grade 4   Read pages 189–192 to discover how the Ten Commandments help us love others as Jesus taught us.

Grade 5   Read pages 197–200 to discover how the Ten Commandments help us live the Great Commandment.

Grade 6   Read pages 189–192 to discover what the Sixth and Ninth Commandments teach us.

Kindergarten Connection
Faith First Kindergarten Chapter 21
Junior High Connection
Faith First Legacy Edition Junior High *Morality: Life in Christ* Chapters 9 and 10 and *Jesus in the New Testament* Chapter 9

Sharing Together

You can use the following questions to discuss what the children have read. Be sure to answer any questions the children may have. Remember that the responses given below are simply one way to express the main idea underlying the response to each question, so be sure to affirm all appropriate responses.

- *How does God ask us to treat other people?*
  (God asks us to respect, love, and honor all people. God asks us to care for and help one another.)

- *How can we keep the Fourth Commandment?*
  (We keep the Fourth Commandment by respecting our parents, who have shared the gift of life and the gift of faith with us. We appreciate all the good our parents do for us. We help our parents and all people who have the responsibility to care for us.)

- *What does the Fifth Commandment teach?*
  (The Fifth Commandment teaches not to kill. All life is sacred and a gift from God. We are to respect and treat everyone as a child of God.)

- *What do the Sixth and Ninth Commandments teach?*
  (The Sixth Commandment teaches not to commit adultery. The Ninth Commandment teaches us not to covet our neighbor's wife. These Commandments teach us to respect our sexuality, to love one another in appropriate ways, and to be pure in mind, heart, and in our actions.)

- *Why are the Seventh, Eighth, and Tenth Commandments important?*
  (The Seventh Commandment teaches not to steal. The Eighth Commandment teaches not to lie or bear false witness. The Tenth Commandment teaches not to covet our neighbor's goods. The Seventh, Eighth, and Tenth Commandments teach about justice, truth, and mercy.)

All Grades Ask the children to share one or two things that they learned from their reading.

Working Together

Choose one of the following activities to do together or design a similar activity of your own.

- Discuss some of the ways that your family lives the Fourth Commandment. What are some ways that each member of your family shows that you care for one another?

- Watch a TV show together. Point out situations in the show that depict the characters living or breaking one of the Ten Commandments. Discuss the consequences of living or breaking the Commandments that were presented on the show.

- Discuss how your family keeps the Seventh Commandment by being good stewards of God's creation. How do you care for the environment? What are some ways your family can improve how it cares for the environment?

- Make Ten Commandment posters. Write each Commandment at the top of a separate sheet of poster paper. Illustrate ways that you can live the Commandment named at the top of each poster. Share your finished posters with one another. Display them in your home as reminders to follow the Commandments.

This week we will . . .

What Difference Does Faith Make?

Provide time for the children to read the "Our Church Makes a Difference" and the "What Difference Does Faith Make in My Life?" pages in their **Faith First Legacy Edition** books and complete the activities on those pages.

Grade 1 Read pages 177 and 178 and ask first graders to share one thing they learned about the Saint Vincent de Paul Society. Have the children share their work and their faith choice on page 178.

Grade 2 Read pages 177 and 178 and ask second graders to share two things that they learned about Saint Vincent de Paul. Have the children share their work and their faith choice on page 178.

Grade 3 Read pages 177 and 178 and ask third graders to share two things that they learned about the parish family. Have the children share their work and their faith choice on page 178.

Grade 4 Read pages 193 and 194 and ask fourth graders to share two things that they learned about L'Arche communities. Have the children share their work and their faith decision on page 194.

Grade 5 Read pages 201 and 202 and ask fifth graders to share two things that they learned about the United States Conference of Catholic Bishops (USCCB). Have the children share their work and their faith decision on page 202.

Grade 6 Read pages 193 and 194 and ask sixth graders to share two things that they learned about Blessed Pope John XXIII and *Pacem in Terris (Peace on Earth)*. Have the children share their work and their faith decision on page 194.

All Grades Discuss ways family members can help one another keep their faith choice or faith decision.

Kindergarten Connection

Ask the children to share what they learned this week.

Junior High Connection

Ask the children to share two things that they learned about loving others. Have the children share their faith decisions.

Praying Together

Ask each child to read and share the prayer page for this chapter of the child's book.

Write each of the last seven Commandments on a separate slip of paper and give the slips of paper to different people. Then gather your family for prayer.

Light a candle and pray.

Leader: Living God,
we are thankful for the time
we have shared today.
Be with us as we pray together.

Reader: (Read aloud Psalm 119:33–34.)

Ask each person to read aloud, one at a time, one of the last seven of the Ten Commandments. After each Commandment is read aloud, the rest of the family responds, "May our love for other people show our love for God."

Leader: God, help us strive each day to live the spirit of your laws. Let us grow in age and wisdom and grace. We ask this through Christ our Lord.

All: Amen.

Be sure to review the "With My Family" page in the child's book. "With My Family" is the last page of each chapter.

Living as the Children of God

The biblical story of creation teaches that God breathed the breath of life into the first human being. This wonderful image reveals the truth of the absolute dependence of humanity on God. Created in God's image and likeness, we are created by God and for God. God's love for us never ceases. God's love for us continually draws us nearer to him.

When we choose to respond to God's love, we choose to live as the children of God. We live as images of God in the world. We announce the good news of God's love to everyone. We are living signs of love and hope.

Using Our Faith First Legacy Edition Books

Use the following chapters to teach this lesson:

Grade 1 · Chapter 15,
      see also Chapters 16 and 17

Grade 2 · Chapter 21,
      see also Chapter 23

Grade 3 · Chapter 21,
      see also Chapters 4 and 10

Grade 4 · Chapter 18,
      see also Chapters 19 and 20

Grade 5 · Chapter 20,
      see also Chapter 21

Grade 6 · Chapter 19,
      see also Chapter 23

Kindergarten Connection
Faith First Kindergarten Chapters 19 and 21
Junior High Connection
Faith First Legacy Edition Junior High
Morality: Life in Christ Chapters 1, 5, and 8 and *Jesus in the New Testament* Chapters 8 and 10

What We Will Learn

Through this lesson your family will learn that:

- God created us to love and know him.
- Scripture, especially the Beatitudes and the Book of Proverbs and the Book of Psalms, helps us live as children of God.
- People teach us how to live as the children of God.

Looking for More?

- **www.FaithFirst.com**
- **Faith First Legacy Edition** *Additional Activities* booklet for appropriate age level
- **Faith First** videos (Gr. 1—segment 3; Gr. 6—segment 3; Junior High *Liturgy and Morality*—segment 8)
- **Faith First Legacy Edition** *Called to Prayer* booklet for appropriate age level
- Video *Francesco's Friendly World*, "The Last Stone"
- Books to read, see pages 16 and 17

Family Blessing

Loving God,
you created us
in your own image and likeness.
Be with us and bless us
as we learn how to
live as your children.
Amen.

PART 1

What We Already Know

Talk with your children to find out what they already know about living as the children of God. You can begin the discussion by using the example below or your own words.

We believe that we are children of God. What do you think it means to be a child of God?

What We Will Discover

Provide time for the children to read and complete the activities.

Grade 1   Read pages 133–136 to discover why God made us.

Grade 2   Read pages 181–184 to discover how the proverbs in the Bible help us live as the children of God.

Grade 3   Read pages 181–184 to discover how praying Psalm 104 can help us live as the children of God.

Grade 4   Read pages 157–160 to discover what the Beatitudes tell us about happiness.

Grade 5   Read pages 173–176 to discover how we live holy lives.

Grade 6   Read pages 165–168 to discover how the Spiritual and Corporal Works of Mercy guide us in living holy lives.

Kindergarten Connection
Faith First Kindergarten Chapters 1, 5, and 22
Junior High Connection
Faith First Legacy Edition Junior High *Morality: Life in Christ* Chapters 1, 5, and 8 and *Jesus in the New Testament* Chapters 8 and 10

Sharing Together

You can use the following questions to discuss what the children have read. Be sure to answer any questions the children may have. Remember that the responses given below are simply one way to express the main idea underlying the response to each question, so be sure to affirm all appropriate responses.

- *How can we live as the children of God?*
  (Anytime we serve God or other people, we are living as the children of God. We are living as the children of God when we live a life based on the values taught and revealed by Jesus Christ.)

- *How does Scripture help us live as the children of God?*
  (Scripture is God's word to us. The Book of Proverbs helps us make wise choices. The Book of Psalms helps us remember to care for creation. The Beatitudes teach us about living a life of true happiness.)

- *Who are the people that teach us how to live as the children of God?*
  (Responses will vary.)

All Grades Ask the children to share one or two things that they learned from their reading.

Working Together

Choose one of the following activities to do together or design a similar activity of your own.

- For one week, keep a family journal of kindness. Make a journal and record the many acts of kindness and love that family members perform each day. If children are old enough, they can write in the journal themselves. Younger children may need a parent to help them. Share the contents of the journal daily or at the end of the week.

- Make a "Children of God" collage or poster. Print the words *Children of God* on a piece of poster board. Create a collage using magazine pictures, or draw pictures that show people living as the children of God. Display the completed work in your home as a reminder to live as the children of God.

- Living as the children of God includes resolving conflicts peacefully. Follow these simple guidelines to help your family resolve conflicts peacefully:
  - Listen to both sides of the story.
  - Restate what was heard.
  - Be open to compromise.
  - Make a fresh start.
  As you use these guidelines, be sure to add to them or change them to fit your family's needs.

- Choose a saint or a modern-day leader in the Church and research the life and work of the person. The Internet or parish library can be a source of information. Find out and discuss how this person lived as a child of God. Talk about how this person can be a guide for your family to live as children of God.

This week we will . . .

_____

_____

_____

_____

What Difference Does Faith Make?

Provide time for the children to read the "Our Church Makes a Difference" and the "What Difference Does Faith Make in My Life?" pages in their **Faith First Legacy Edition** books and complete the activities on those pages.

Grade 1 Read pages 137 and 138 and ask first graders to share one thing they learned about Saint Katharine Drexel. Have the children share their work and their faith choice on page 138.

Grade 2 Read pages 185 and 186 and ask second graders to share two things that they learned about Christian sayings. Have the children share their work and their faith choice on page 186.

Grade 3 Read pages 185 and 186 and ask third graders to share two things that they learned about farmers. Have the children share their work and their faith choice on page 186.

Grade 4 Read pages 161 and 162 and ask fourth graders to share two things that they learned about Saint Francis of Assisi. Have the children share their work and their faith decision on page 162.

Grade 5 Read pages 177 and 178 and ask fifth graders to share two things that they learned about Father Solanus Casey. Have the children share their work and their faith decision on page 178.

Grade 6 Read pages 169 and 170 and ask sixth graders to share two things that they learned about the work of the Gleaners. Have the children share their work and their faith decision on page 170.

All Grades Discuss ways family members can help one another keep their faith choice or faith decision.

Kindergarten Connection
Ask the children to share what they learned this week.

Junior High Connection
Ask the children to share two things that they learned about living as the children of God. Have the children share their faith decisions.

Praying Together

Ask each child to read and share the prayer page for this chapter of the child's book.

Use a candle that you can safely pass from one person to another during the prayer. Gather your family for prayer.

Light the candle and pray.

Leader: Living God,
we are thankful for the time
we have shared today.
Be with us as we pray together.

Reader: (Read aloud Psalm 139:1–6, 13–16.)

Pass the candle from one person to another. As each person holds the candle, the rest of the family says, "*(Name)*, may you grow in holiness and live as a child of God."

The person holding the candle responds, "Amen."

Leader: God, help us remember always to serve you and one another so that we may live as your children. We ask this through Christ our Lord.

All: Amen.

Be sure to review the "With My Family" page in the child's book. "With My Family" is the last page of each chapter.

Making Choices

God has given us the special gifts of free will and conscience. By giving us these gifts, God has placed the responsibility for loving him in our hands. God has given us the freedom to cooperate with his grace and make the choice to grow closer to him or away from him. The choice is ours to make. We can choose to turn toward God and respond to his love; OR we can turn away from God and chase fame, riches, and pleasure instead.

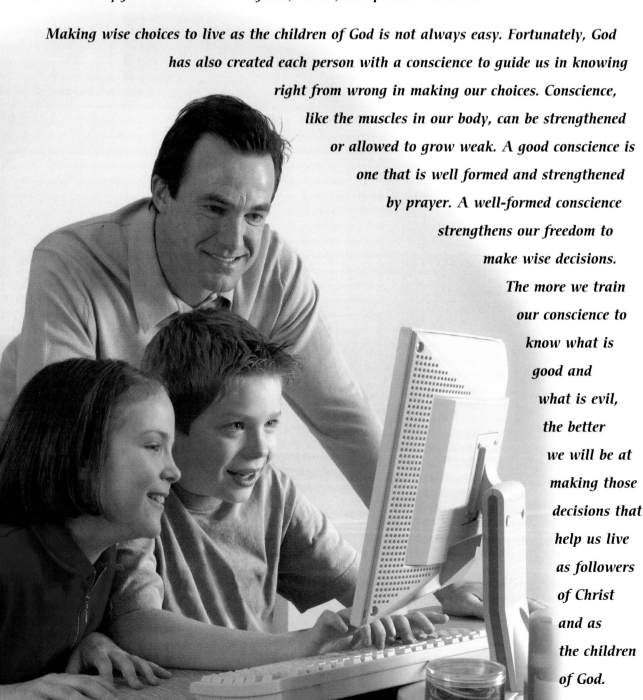

Making wise choices to live as the children of God is not always easy. Fortunately, God has also created each person with a conscience to guide us in knowing right from wrong in making our choices. Conscience, like the muscles in our body, can be strengthened or allowed to grow weak. A good conscience is one that is well formed and strengthened by prayer. A well-formed conscience strengthens our freedom to make wise decisions. The more we train our conscience to know what is good and what is evil, the better we will be at making those decisions that help us live as followers of Christ and as the children of God.

Using Our Faith First Legacy Edition Books

Use the following chapters to teach this lesson:

Grade 1 · Chapter 21

Grade 2 · Chapter 22

Grade 3 · Chapter 22

Grade 4 · Chapter 17

Grade 5 · Chapter 18

Grade 6 · Chapter 20

Kindergarten Connection

Faith First Kindergarten Chapter 19

Junior High Connection

Faith First Legacy Edition Junior High *Morality: Life in Christ* Chapters 2, 3, and 11

What We Will Learn

Through this lesson your family will learn that:

■ Jesus taught us how to make wise choices.

■ Our conscience helps us know right and wrong.

■ We are responsible for our choices.

Looking for More?

■ www.FaithFirst.com

■ **Faith First Legacy Edition** *Additional Activities* booklet for appropriate age level

■ **Faith First** videos (Grade 4— segment 5; Grade 6—segment 5)

■ **Faith First Legacy Edition** *Called to Prayer* booklet for appropriate age level

■ Books to read, see pages 16 and 17

Family Blessing

Loving God,
be with us and bless us
as we learn
how to make wise choices
that show our love
for you and for one another.
Amen.

PART 1

What We Already Know

Talk with your children to find out what they already know about making choices. You can begin the discussion by using the example below or your own words.

Jesus taught us how to make wise choices. Making wise choices shows God that we love him. Let's share with one another some of the wise choices that we have made.

What We Will Discover

Provide time for the children to read and complete the activities.

Grade 1   Read pages 181–184 to discover ways we ask for forgiveness.

Grade 2   Read pages 189–192 to discover how we can make wise choices.

Grade 3   Read pages 189–192 to discover what grace is.

Grade 4   Read pages 149–152 to discover why we are responsible for our choices and their consequences.

Grade 5   Read pages 157–160 to discover what we need to do to correctly form a moral conscience.

Grade 6   Read pages 173–176 to discover where we can find guidance for making moral decisions.

Kindergarten Connection

Faith First Kindergarten Chapter 19

Junior High Connection

Faith First Legacy Edition Junior High *Morality: Life in Christ* Chapters 2, 3, and 11

Sharing Together

You can use the following questions to discuss what the children have read. Be sure to answer any questions the children may have. Remember that the responses given below are simply one way to express the main idea underlying the response to each question, so be sure to affirm all appropriate responses.

■ *Why is it important to make wise choices?*
(Making wise choices shows our love for God, other people, and ourselves.)

■ *How do we make wise choices?*
(In order to make wise choices we need to stop and think and pray about what we are choosing. We need to ask whether the choice shows our love for God, for ourselves, and for others. We need to correctly form and listen to our conscience.)

■ *What is conscience?*
(Conscience is the gift from God that helps us know and judge what is right and what is wrong.)

■ *What is sin?*
(Sin is freely choosing to say or do something that we know is against God's Law. Sin sets itself against God's love for us and turns our hearts away from God's love.)

All Grades Ask the children to share one or two things that they learned from their reading.

Working Together

Choose one of the following activities to do together or design a similar activity of your own.

■ Watch a TV program as a family. As you are viewing the program, look for situations that portray one of the characters making a wise choice or a bad choice. Then discuss the choice that was made as well as other decisions that could have been made in the situation.

■ Work together to make two lists of choices. On one piece of paper, list choices that bring us closer to God. On another piece of paper, list choices that turn us away from God's love. Talk about why the choices are wise choices or bad choices.

■ Talk about ways you can help one another make wise choices. Write all your ideas on a piece of paper and post the list in a place in your home where it can be seen by everyone. The list will serve as a reminder of the importance of making morally good choices.

■ Make a "Conscience Banner" out of poster paper. At the top of a piece of poster paper, write the words *Forming a Good Conscience*. Below the heading draw pictures or write phrases that describe ways we can develop a well-formed conscience. You might also like to include some Scripture verses that encourage people to act wisely.

This week we will . . .

_____

_____

_____

_____

_____

_____

What Difference Does Faith Make?

Provide time for the children to read the "Our Church Makes a Difference" and the "What Difference Does Faith Make in My Life?" pages in their **Faith First Legacy Edition** books and complete the activities on those pages.

Grade 1 Read pages 185 and 186 and ask first graders to share one thing they learned about Pope John Paul II. Have the children share their work and their faith choice on page 186.

Grade 2 Read pages 193 and 194 and ask second graders to share two things that they learned about morning and night prayers. Have the children share their work and their faith choice on page 194.

Grade 3 Read pages 193 and 194 and ask third graders to share two things that they learned about the Funeral Mass. Have the children share their work and their faith choice on page 194.

Grade 4 Read pages 153 and 154 and ask fourth graders to share two things that they learned about Saint Augustine. Have the children share their work and their faith decision on page 154.

Grade 5 Read pages 161 and 162 and ask fifth graders to share two things that they learned about retreats. Have the children share their work and their faith decision on page 162.

Grade 6 Read pages 177 and 178 and ask sixth graders to share two things that they learned about Saint John Bosco. Have the children share their work and their faith decision on page 178.

All Grades Discuss ways family members can help one another keep their faith choice or faith decision.

Kindergarten Connection
Ask the children to share what they learned this week.

Junior High Connection
Ask the children to share two things that they learned about making wise choices. Have the children share their faith decisions.

Praying Together

Ask each child to read and share the prayer page for this chapter of the child's book.

Find a Bible to use for prayer. Then gather your family for prayer.

Light a candle and pray.

Leader: Living God,
we are thankful for the time
we have shared today.
Be with us as we pray together.

Reader: (Read aloud Psalm 25:8–12.)

Pass the Bible from one person to another. As each person holds the Bible, everyone else says, "Holy Spirit, help *(Name)* to make wise decisions to live as a follower of Jesus."

The person holding the Bible responds, "Amen."

Leader: God our loving Father, send us the Holy Spirit to help us strengthen and follow our conscience. We ask this through Christ our Lord.

All: Amen.

Be sure to review the "With My Family" page in the child's book. "With My Family" is the last page of each chapter.

People of Prayer

Prayer is a vital link with our Creator. It is vital to living our relationship with God the Father, God the Son, and God the Holy Spirit. Transformed by the love of God, we long to respond to God's gracious love. One way we respond to that love is by communicating with God and opening our hearts to further transformation through prayer.

Christians are joined to Christ in Baptism. In our prayer Jesus joins us, the Holy Spirit moves us and teaches us to pray, and the Father listens with loving care.

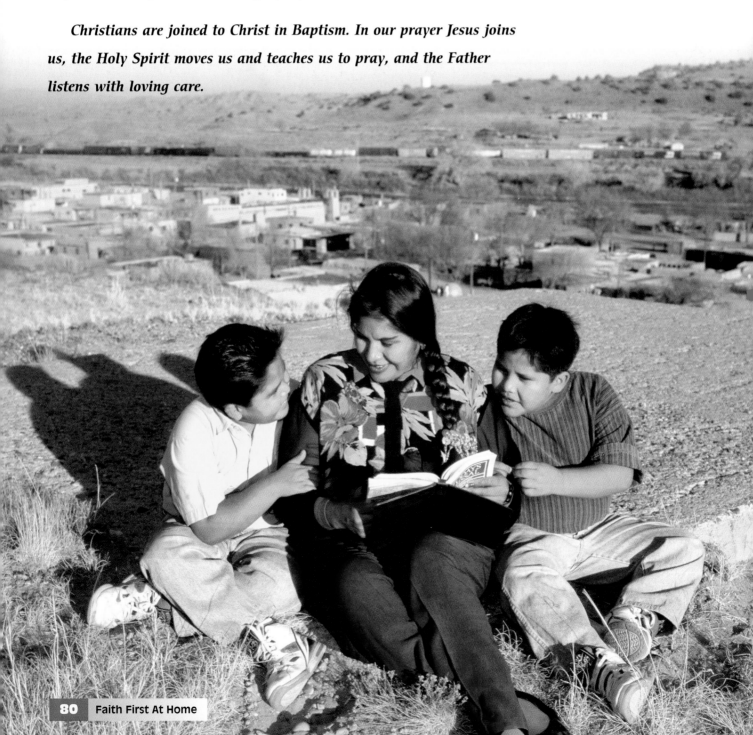

Using Our Faith First Legacy Edition Books

Use the following chapters to teach this lesson:

Grade 1 · Chapter 23

Grade 2 · Chapter 24,
see also chapter 11

Grade 3 · Chapter 25

Grade 4 · Chapter 24

Grade 5 · Chapter 24

Grade 6 · Chapter 24

Kindergarten Connection
Have your child work with another child for this lesson.

Junior High Connection
Faith First Legacy Edition Junior High
Church and Sacraments Chapter 14

What We Will Learn

Through this lesson your family will learn that:

■ Prayer is talking and listening to God.

■ Jesus showed us how to pray.

■ We can pray anytime and anywhere.

■ The Holy Spirit teaches and helps us pray.

■ We can grow as people of prayer.

Looking for More?

■ **www.FaithFirst.com**

■ **Faith First Legacy Edition** *Additional Activities* booklet for appropriate age level

■ **Faith First** videos (Grade 3—segment 7; Grade 5—segment 7)

■ **Faith First Legacy Edition** *Called to Prayer* booklet for appropriate age level

■ Books to read, see pages 16 and 17

Family Blessing

*Loving Creator,
be with us and bless us
as we learn more about
how we can talk and listen to you
through prayer.
Amen.*

PART 1

 ## What We Already Know

Talk with your children to find out what they already know about prayer. You can begin the discussion by using the example below or your own words.

We believe that prayer is talking and listening to God. Let's share with one another the ways and the times that we pray.

 ## What We Will Discover

Provide time for the children to read and complete the activities.

Grade 1 Read pages 201–204 to discover why it is important to pray.

Grade 2 Read pages 209–212 to discover why it is important to pray many times during the day.

Grade 3 Read pages 217–220 to discover that the Holy Spirit teaches us to pray.

Grade 4 Read pages 209–212 to discover what we do when we pray.

Grade 5 Read pages 209–212 to discover how praying was a part of Jesus' life.

Grade 6 Read pages 209–212 to discover how we can improve our life of prayer.

Kindergarten Connection
Have your child work with another child for this lesson.

Junior High Connection
Faith First Legacy Edition Junior High *Church and Sacraments* Chapter 14

Sharing Together

You can use the following questions to discuss what the children have read. Be sure to answer any questions the children may have. Remember that the responses given below are simply one way to express the main idea underlying the response to each question, so be sure to affirm all appropriate responses.

■ *What is prayer?*
(Prayer is talking and listening to God. Prayer is spending time with God and enjoying his company.)

■ *Why is prayer important?*
(Praying is a sign of our faith and trust in God. It is a sign of our love for God.)

■ *What did Jesus teach us about prayer?*
(Jesus taught us that we are to place our trust in God the Father above all else. Jesus taught that we can pray alone or with others and that we can pray anywhere and anytime.)

■ *Why do we believe that God always listens to our prayers?*
(Jesus taught us that God listens to our prayers.)

All Grades Ask the children to share one or two things that they learned from their reading.

Working Together

Choose one of the following activities to do together or design a similar activity of your own.

■ Take a family prayer walk. Go for a walk together and thank God for all the things you see and hear. You can stop anytime during your walk and say a short prayer.

■ This week pray the Apostles' Creed or the Nicene Creed as a family. Work together to memorize one of these creeds of the Church. Talk about the truths of our faith that are summarized in these creeds. Explain that the creeds are some of the great prayers of the Church.

■ Read one or several of these passages about prayer from Luke's account of the Gospel:
• Luke 3:21–22 (The Baptism of Jesus)
• Luke 6:12–13 (The Mission of the Twelve)
• Luke 9:28–29 (The Transfiguration of Jesus)
• Luke 22:32 (Peter's Denial of Jesus Foretold)
• Luke 22:41–42 (The Agony in the Garden)
• Luke 23:46 (The Death of Jesus)

Talk about how Jesus helps us grow as people of prayer.

■ Discuss ways you can pray together as a family. Choose one day each week when you will pray together. Talk about how you will get ready for prayer and some of the ways you can pray.

This week we will . . .

_____

_____

_____

_____

_____

_____

What Difference Does Faith Make?

Provide time for the children to read the "Our Church Makes a Difference" and the "What Difference Does Faith Make in My Life?" pages in their **Faith First Legacy Edition** books and complete the activities on those pages.

Grade 1 Read pages 205 and 206 and ask first graders to share one thing that they learned about prayer partners. Have the children share their work and their faith choice on page 206.

Grade 2 Read pages 213 and 214 and ask second graders to share two things that they learned about Blessed Kateri Tekakwitha. Have the children share their work and their faith choice on page 214.

Grade 3 Read pages 221 and 222 and ask third graders to share two things that they learned about actions speaking louder than words. Have the children share their work and their faith choice on page 222.

Grade 4 Read pages 213 and 214 and ask fourth graders to share two things that they learned about prayer partners. Have the children share their work and their faith decision on page 214.

Grade 5 Read pages 213 and 214 and ask fifth graders to share two things that they learned about Christian role models. Have the children share their work and their faith decision on page 214.

Grade 6 Read pages 213 and 214 and ask sixth graders to share two things that they learned about the Jesus Prayer. Have the children share their work and their faith decision on page 214.

All Grades Discuss ways family members can help one another keep their faith choice or faith decision.

Kindergarten Connection

Ask the children to share what they learned this week.

Junior High Connection

Ask the children to share two things that they learned about Christian prayer. Have the children share their faith decisions.

Praying Together

Ask each child to read and share the prayer page for this chapter of the child's book.

Give everyone a few minutes to write a prayer of petition. Remind everyone to end the petition with the words "We pray to the Lord." When everyone has finished writing their petitions, gather your family for prayer.

Light a candle and pray.

Leader: Loving God,
we are thankful for the time
we have shared today.
Be with us as we pray together.

Reader: (Read aloud Philippians 4:4–7.)

Ask each person to pray their petition aloud. After each person prays their petition, the rest of the family responds, "Lord, hear our prayer."

Leader: God, help us remember to pray always and everywhere. We ask this through Christ our Lord.

All: Amen.

Be sure to review the "With My Family" page in the child's book. "With My Family" is the last page of each chapter.

Ways of Praying

Jesus taught us that we are to pray. Praying is one of the ways we express and deepen our relationship with God. Prayer has many dimensions. Prayer is an expression of our thirst for God. Through prayer we open our hearts in gratitude to God for his generosity to us. Praying is also a source of strength when we face temptation and evil. In prayer we surrender our struggles to God. Ultimately, praying is our communion with God, who has created us and breathed the gift of his own life into us.

The Church names five basic types of prayer. They are the prayer of blessing and adoration, the prayer of petition, the prayer of intercession, the prayer of thanksgiving, and the prayer of praise. Often our prayer is a mix of several of these types of prayer.

Praying is itself a gift from God. We cannot pray on our own. The Holy Spirit within us urges us to pray and teaches us to pray. The Holy Spirit moves us to express our prayers and to listen to God speaking to us. Praying is so vital to our life that we must pray without ceasing.

Using Our Faith First Legacy Edition Books

Use the following chapters to teach this lesson:

Grade 1 · Chapter 25,
            see also chapter 24

Grade 2 · Chapter 25

Grade 3 · Chapter 24

Grade 4 · Chapter 25

Grade 5 · Chapter 25

Grade 6 · Chapter 25

Kindergarten Connection
Faith First Kindergarten Chapter 24
Junior High Connection
Faith First Legacy Edition Junior High
Church and Sacraments Chapter 5

What We Will Learn

Through this lesson your family will learn that:

- There are many ways to pray.
- Our body posture and actions can help us pray.
- The different types of prayer include prayers of petition, intercession, thanksgiving, blessing, and praise.
- Prayer expresses our belief and trust in God.

Looking for More?

- www.FaithFirst.com
- **Faith First Legacy Edition** *Additional Activities* booklet for appropriate age level
- **Faith First** videos (Grade 3— segment 7; Grade 5—segment 1)
- **Faith First Legacy Edition** *Called to Prayer* booklet for appropriate age level
- Books to read, see pages 16 and 17

Family Blessing

Loving God,
be with us and bless us.
Help us listen as you speak to us,
and help us hear your words.
Amen.

PART 1

What We Already Know

Talk with your children to find out what they already know about prayer. You can begin the discussion by using the example below or your own words.

We can use our hands, our arms, and our voices to pray. We can pray alone or with others. Let's share with one another some of the ways we pray.

What We Will Discover

Provide time for the children to read and complete the activities.

Grade 1 Read pages 217–220 to discover why singing is a form of prayer.

Grade 2 Read pages 217–220 to discover how Jesus taught us to pray.

Grade 3 Read pages 209–212 to discover why we say thank-you to God.

Grade 4 Read pages 217–220 to discover the ways Christians express our prayers to God.

Grade 5 Read pages 217–220 to discover why Catholics pray with and to Mary.

Grade 6 Read pages 217–220 to discover how we pray a prayer of meditation.

Kindergarten Connection
Faith First Kindergarten Chapter 24
Junior High Connection
Faith First Legacy Edition Junior High *Church and Sacraments* Chapter 5

Sharing Together

You can use the following questions to discuss what the children have read. Be sure to answer any questions the children may have. Remember that the responses given below are simply one way to express the main idea underlying the response to each question, so be sure to affirm all appropriate responses.

■ *What are some actions that help us pray?*
(Some prayer actions include making the sign of the cross, genuflecting, kneeling, standing, bowing our heads, closing our eyes, holding one another's hands, and folding our hands.)

■ *What are some of the different types of prayers?*
(There are prayers of thanksgiving, praise, intercession, petition, and adoration and blessing.)

■ *What is a prayer of thanksgiving?*
(A prayer of thanksgiving gives thanks to God for the gift of creation, for our salvation in Jesus Christ, for the gift of holiness, and for every blessing.)

■ *What is a prayer of praise?*
(A prayer of praise tells God that we believe he alone is God. There is only one God. We love him above everyone and everything else. He has done good things for us that no one else could ever do.)

■ *What is a prayer of intercession?*
(A prayer of intercession asks God to help others. We pray that all people may know God's love for them.)

■ *What is a prayer of petition?*
(A prayer of petition asks God for forgiveness and for help in all our needs.)

■ *What is a prayer of adoration and blessing?*
(A prayer of adoration and blessing acknowledges God to be the Creator. God gives us the gift of life and shares his life and love with us.)

All Grades Ask the children to share one or two things that they learned from their reading.

Working Together

Choose one of the following activities to do together or design a similar activity of your own.

■ Write a family blessing prayer together. Pray the blessing before meals, at the end of each day, or on special occasions.

■ Find out more about the prayer ministry of your parish. Talk to your priest or another pastoral minister, or look in the parish bulletin. Find out how people can include prayer requests in your parish's prayer network. Talk to one of the volunteers who takes part in the prayer network about the importance of your parish's prayer ministry.

■ Pray a mantra. A mantra consists of one word or a short phrase that is prayed over and over again in rhythm with a slow breathing pattern. For example, you may choose as a mantra "Jesus, be with me." Pray the word "Jesus" silently as you inhale, and the words "be with me" as you exhale. Breathe slowly and continue praying the mantra for a few minutes. Afterward, talk about how praying a mantra can help us feel closer to God and more at peace.

■ When we practice a skill or consciously repeat the same action over and over, that action becomes a habit. Make a list of good habits for prayer. Talk about ways that you can try to develop these prayer habits together.

This week we will . . .

_____

_____

_____

_____

_____

What Difference Does Faith Make?

Provide time for the children to read the "Our Church Makes a Difference" and the "What Difference Does Faith Make in My Life?" pages in their **Faith First Legacy Edition** books and complete the activities on those pages.

Grade 1 Read pages 221 and 222 and ask first graders to share one thing that they learned about Sister Thea Bowman. Have the children share their work and their faith choice on page 222.

Grade 2 Read pages 221 and 222 and ask second graders to share two things that they learned about people who live a life of prayer. Have the children share their work and their faith choice on page 222.

Grade 3 Read pages 213 and 214 and ask third graders to share two things that they learned about prayer groups. Have the children share their work and their faith choice on page 214.

Grade 4 Read pages 221 and 222 and ask fourth graders to share two things that they learned about pilgrimages. Have the children share their work and their faith decision on page 222.

Grade 5 Read pages 221 and 222 and ask fifth graders to share two things that they learned about people of prayer. Have the children share their work and their faith decision on page 222.

Grade 6 Read pages 221 and 222 and ask sixth graders to share two things that they learned about Saint Hildegard of Bingen. Have the children share their work and their faith decision on page 222.

All Grades Discuss ways family members can help one another keep their faith choice or faith decision.

Kindergarten Connection
Ask the children to share what they learned this week.
Junior High Connection
Ask the children to share two things that they learned about different forms of prayer. Have the children share their faith decisions.

Praying Together

Ask each child to read and share the prayer page for this chapter of the child's book.

Give everyone a few minutes to write down some things that they are thankful to God for. Then gather your family for prayer.

Light a candle and pray.

Leader: God our Father,
we are thankful for the time
we have shared today.
Be with us as we pray together.

Ask each person to say, "I am thankful for _____." After each person expresses their thanks to God, the rest of the family responds, "We bless you, O Lord."

Leader: God, help us remember to always give you thanks and praise. We ask this through Christ our Lord.

All: Amen.

Be sure to review the "With My Family" page in the child's book. "With My Family" is the last page of each chapter.

The Lord's Prayer

The Our Father is a summary of the whole Gospel. When we pray the Our Father, we express our desire to love God the Father in both our words and deeds and to emulate his loving-kindness. By addressing God as Father, we acknowledge our dignity as adopted sons and daughters of God—a dignity that no one can ever take from us.

We have all prayed the Our Father, or the Lord's Prayer, many times. Its words spring forth from our memory and onto our lips so quickly that our hearts and minds may easily be bypassed. The words of the Our Father are so familiar that the recitation of the Lord's Prayer may become routine and mechanical and its awesome importance may elude us.

Jesus could have chosen any words to teach us to pray. He chose "Our Father . . ." These were the words that flowed from his love for the Father and us. Jesus invites us to address God the Father as Abba and to place our trust unconditionally in the Father as he himself did.

Using Our Faith First Legacy Edition Books

Use the following chapters to teach this lesson:

Grade 1 · Chapter 26
Grade 2 · Chapter 26
Grade 3 · Chapter 23
Grade 4 · Chapter 26
Grade 5 · Chapter 26
Grade 6 · Chapter 26

Kindergarten Connection
Faith First Kindergarten Chapter 24
Junior High Connection
Faith First Legacy Edition Junior High
Morality: Life in Christ Chapter 12

What We Will Learn

Through this lesson your family will learn that:

■ Jesus taught us the Our Father, or the Lord's Prayer.

■ The Our Father teaches us how to pray.

■ The Our Father teaches us how to live.

Looking for More?

■ **www.FaithFirst.com**

■ **Faith First Legacy Edition** *Additional Activities* booklet for appropriate age level

■ **Faith First** videos (Grade 3— segment 8; Grade 5—segment 7)

■ **Faith First Legacy Edition** *Called to Prayer* booklet for appropriate age level

■ Books to read, see pages 16 and 17

Family Blessing

God our Father,
help us pray the Lord's Prayer
as Jesus did
with all our heart,
with all our mind,
and with all our soul.
Amen.

PART 1

 ## What We Already Know

Talk with your children to find out what they already know about the Lord's Prayer. You can begin the discussion by using the example below or your own words.

We believe that Jesus taught us the Lord's Prayer, or the Our Father. When are some of the times we pray the Our Father?

 ## What We Will Discover

Provide time for the children to read and complete the activities.

Grade 1   Read pages 225–228 to discover what Jesus teaches us about prayer.

Grade 2   Read pages 225–228 to discover ways that we live the Our Father.

Grade 3   Read pages 201–204 to discover ways that Jesus teaches us to pray.

Grade 4   Read pages 225–228 to discover what Jesus teaches us in the Our Father.

Grade 5   Read pages 225–228 to discover the meaning of the words of the Our Father.

Grade 6   Read pages 225–228 to discover why the Lord's Prayer is a prayer of trust in God.

Kindergarten Connection
Faith First Kindergarten Chapter 24
Junior High Connection
Faith First Legacy Edition Junior High *Morality: Life in Christ* Chapter 20

Sharing Together

You can use the following questions to discuss what the children have read. Be sure to answer any questions the children may have. Remember that the responses given below are simply one way to express the main idea underlying the response to each question, so be sure to affirm all appropriate responses.

- *What does Jesus teach us about prayer?* (Jesus teaches us that we are to pray to God as our Father. We can pray anywhere and anytime.)

- *How does the Lord's Prayer, or the Our Father, teach us how to live?* (When we pray the Lord's Prayer, we ask God to forgive us, to help us make good choices, and to live as children of God.)

- *What is the meaning of the Lord's Prayer?* (We praise God's name. We ask God to continue to build the kingdom of God. We promise to live as Jesus taught us. We ask for all we need to live as the children of God. We ask God to forgive us and to help us forgive others. We ask God to help us live according to his will and avoid doing wrong.)

All Grades Ask the children to share one or two things that they learned from their reading.

Working Together

Choose one of the following activities to do together or design a similar activity of your own.

- Make an Our Father puzzle. Write the words to the Our Father on a piece of paper. Cut out each line of the prayer into puzzle pieces. See how long it takes to put the prayer puzzle pieces back together.

- Make an Our Father booklet. Read the Our Father and write each phrase of the Our Father on a page in the booklet. Write or draw ways your family can live each part of the Our Father.

- All Christians pray the Our Father. See if you can find and learn the Our Father in a language other than your own.

- Make up gestures or actions to go with the words of the Our Father. Pray the Our Father together using these gestures or actions.

This week we will . . .

_____

_____

_____

_____

_____

_____

_____

_____

What Difference Does Faith Make?

Provide time for the children to read the "Our Church Makes a Difference" and the "What Difference Does Faith Make in My Life?" pages in their **Faith First Legacy Edition** books and complete the activities on those pages.

Grade 1 Read pages 229 and 230 and ask first graders to share one thing that they learned about Blessed Teresa of Calcutta. Have the children share their work and their faith choice on page 230.

Grade 2 Read pages 229 and 230 and ask second graders to share two things that they learned about what it means to say that we belong to God's family. Have the children share their work and their faith choice on page 230.

Grade 3 Read pages 205 and 206 and ask third graders to share two things that they learned about objects that help us pray. Have the children share their work and their faith choice on page 206.

Grade 4 Read pages 229 and 230 and ask fourth graders to share two things that they learned about the Heifer Project. Have the children share their work and their faith decision on page 230.

Grade 5 Read pages 229 and 230 and ask fifth graders to share two things that they learned about being stewards of God's creation. Have the children share their work and their faith decision on page 230.

Grade 6 Read pages 229 and 230 and ask sixth graders to share two things that they learned about evangelization. Have the children share their work and their faith decision on page 230.

All Grades Discuss ways family members can help one another keep their faith choice or faith decision.

Kindergarten Connection
Ask the children to share what they learned this week.
Junior High Connection
Ask the children to share two things that they learned about the Our Father. Have the children share their faith decisions.

Praying Together

Ask each child to read and share the prayer page for this chapter of the child's book.

Gather your family for prayer.

Light a candle and pray.

Leader: God our Creator,
we are thankful for the time
we have shared today.
Be with us as we pray together.

Reader: (Read aloud Matthew 6:7–13.)

All: Join hands and pray the Lord's Prayer aloud together. Conclude by sharing a sign of peace with one another.

Leader: God, help us remember to always pray as Jesus taught us. We ask this through Christ our Lord.

All: Amen.

Be sure to review the "With My Family" page in the child's book. "With My Family" is the last page of each chapter.

Mary

Christians honor Mary because God has given her a privileged place in his plan of salvation. Mary is the Mother of God; the mother of Jesus, the Incarnate Son of God; and the mother of the Church. Mary has been honored by God in ways no other human persons have been. If we think these honors make her unapproachable, we miss Mary's significance for our lives. She is our mother too!

Mary was a wife and a mother. Her life on earth is a model of how to balance the demands of spiritual life, married life, and motherhood. Mary is revered by the Church as our great model of faith, hope, and charity. She listened, she freely believed, and she generously said yes to God. Her willingness to trust in God and to seek to know and live God's will shows us how we are to live.

Using Our Faith First Legacy Edition Books

Use the following chapters to teach this lesson:

Grade 1 · Chapter 3

Grade 2 · Chapter 10, pages 88–91

Grade 3 · Chapter 3

Grade 4 · Chapter 6, page 54

Grade 5 · Chapter 6, pages 55–58

Grade 6 · Chapter 9

Kindergarten Connection
Faith First Kindergarten pages 153, 154, 171, and 172
Junior High Connection
Faith First Legacy Edition Junior High *Mystery of God* Chapter 6, pages 64–67

What We Will Learn

Through this lesson your family will learn that:

- Mary is the Mother of God, the mother of Jesus, and the mother of the Church.
- Mary is a model of faith.
- The Church celebrates feasts to honor Mary.
- Mary helps us live as the children of God.

Looking for More?

- **www.FaithFirst.com**
- **Faith First Legacy Edition** *Additional Activities* booklet for appropriate age level
- **Faith First Legacy Edition** *Called to Prayer* booklet for appropriate age level
- Books to read, see pages 16 and 17

Family Blessing

Loving God,
be with us and bless us.
Help us trust in you
and open our hearts
to hear you.
Amen.

PART 1

What We Already Know

Talk with your children to find out what they already know about Mary. You can begin the discussion by using the example below or your own words.

Mary is the Mother of God. She is the mother of Jesus, who is true God and true man; and she is the mother of the Church. Let's share with one another what we already know about Mary.

What We Will Discover

Provide time for the children to read and complete the activities.

Grade 1   Read pages 37–40 to discover how Mary showed her love for God.

Grade 2   Read page 88 to learn the Hail Mary.

Grade 3   Read pages 29–32 to discover how Mary showed her faith and trust in God.

Grade 4   Read page 54 to discover how God kept his promise to send the world the Savior.

Grade 5   Read pages 55 and 56 to discover why we call Mary the Mother of God.

Grade 6   Read pages 77–80 to discover ways that we show our devotion to Mary.

Kindergarten Connection
Faith First Kindergarten pages 153, 154, 171, and 172
Junior High Connection
Faith First Legacy Edition Junior High *Mystery of God* Chapter 6, pages 64–67

Sharing Together

You can use the following questions to discuss what the children have read. Be sure to answer any questions the children may have. Remember that the responses given below are simply one way to express the main idea underlying the response to each question, so be sure to affirm all appropriate responses.

■ *Why do we honor Mary as Mother of God?*
(Mary is the mother of Jesus, who is true God and true man.)

■ *Why do we honor Mary as mother of the Church?*
(In the Gospel according to John we read that Jesus asked John to care for his mother and Mary to care for John. This story tells us that Mary is the mother of all who believe in and follow her Son.)

■ *Why do we pray to Mary?*
(Mary lives in heaven. We pray to honor Mary. In prayer we honor Mary as the Mother of God. We ask Mary, our mother, to pray for us and help us.)

All Grades Ask the children to share one or two things that they learned from their reading.

 ## Working Together

Choose one of the following activities to do together or design a similar activity of your own.

■ Learn the Hail Mary or how to pray the Rosary. Look in the "Catholic Prayers and Practices" section of the children's **Faith First Legacy Edition** books for an explanation of the Rosary.

■ Ask parents or older relatives to share ways that they showed their honor to Mary when they were young. Think of a way you as a family can honor Mary.

■ Saint Dominic and Saint Bernadette are two saints that had great devotion to Mary. See if you can find out more about these two saints or any other saints and their devotion to Mary.

■ The next time you go to Mass, point out to your children the statue of Mary in your parish church. Discuss why there is a special place for Mary in all Catholic churches.

This week we will . . .

What Difference Does Faith Make?

Provide time for the children to read the "Our Church Makes a Difference" and the "What Difference Does Faith Make in My Life?" pages in their **Faith First Legacy Edition** books and complete the activities on those pages.

Grade 1 Read pages 41 and 42 and ask first graders to share one thing that they learned about churches named after Mary. Have the children share their work and their faith choice on page 42.

Grade 2 Read pages 89 and 90 and ask second graders to share two things that they learned about Mary and the saints. Have the children share their work and their faith choice on page 90.

Grade 3 Read pages 33 and 34 and ask third graders to share two things that they learned about the ways the Catholic Church honors Mary. Have the children share their work and their faith choice on page 34.

Grade 4 Have your child work with another child.

Grade 5 Read pages 57 and 58 and ask fifth graders to share two things that they learned about the "Madonna and Child." Have the children share their work and their faith decision on page 58.

Grade 6 Read pages 81 and 82 and ask sixth graders to share two things they learned about the feasts of Mary. Have the children share their work and their faith decision on page 82.

All Grades Discuss ways family members can help one another keep their faith choice or faith decision.

Kindergarten Connection
Ask the children to share what they learned this week.

Junior High Connection
Ask the children to share two things that they learned about the saints and the Blessed Virgin Mary. Have the children share their faith decisions.

Praying Together

Ask each child to read and share the prayer page for this chapter of the child's book.

Find an object in your home that symbolizes Mary, such as a rosary, a picture, or a statue. Gather your family for prayer.

Light a candle and pray.

Leader: God our Creator,
we are thankful for the time
we have shared today.
Be with us as we pray together.

Reader: (Read aloud Luke 1:26–38.)

Pass the symbol of Mary that you have chosen from one person to another. As each person holds the symbol, the rest of the family says, "(Name), may you say yes to God as Mary did."

Pray the Hail Mary together.

Leader: God, help us remember to always trust in you and to respond to your love by doing your will. We ask this through Christ our Lord.

All: Amen.

Be sure to review the "With My Family" page in the child's book. "With My Family" is the last page of each chapter.

The Early Followers of Jesus

The Church is the People of God, the Body of Christ, the temple of the Holy Spirit. Saint Augustine described the work of the Holy Spirit in the Church. He wrote, "What the soul is to the human body, the Holy Spirit is to the Body of Christ." The Holy Spirit empowers the Church community to observe and call the gifts of all members of the Body of Christ into service for the benefit of the whole Church.

Living as followers of Christ involves taking responsibility to develop and use the gifts and talents the Holy Spirit so generously bestows on us. We can discover what it means to live as Christians when we read about the early Church in the New Testament. When our faith in Jesus leads us, as it led the early Christians, to the service of the community, we are manifesting our unity with Christ and with one another. Serving others as Christ did is an ongoing, lifelong commitment that draws us closer and closer to Christ.

Using Our Faith First Legacy Edition Books

Use the following chapters to teach this lesson:

Grade 1 · Chapter 9
Grade 2 · Chapter 8
Grade 3 · Chapter 9
Grade 4 · Chapter 1
Grade 5 · Chapter 15
Grade 6 · Chapter 6

Kindergarten Connection
Faith First Kindergarten Have your child work with another child for this lesson.

Junior High Connection
Faith First Legacy Edition Junior High *Church and Sacraments* Chapter 3, *Morality: Life in Christ* Chapter 4, and *Jesus in the New Testament* Chapter 7

What We Will Learn

Through this lesson your family will learn that:

- Stories about the first Christians are found in the New Testament.
- The first Christians showed how much they loved God and one another.
- Living as Christians includes sharing with, caring for, and loving one another.
- The early Church and the Church today have much in common.

Looking for More?

- www.FaithFirst.com
- **Faith First Legacy Edition** *Additional Activities* booklet for appropriate age level
- **Faith First Legacy Edition** *Called to Prayer* booklet for appropriate age level
- **Faith First** videos (Junior High *Liturgy and Morality*—segment 2)
- Books to read, see pages 16 and 17

Family Blessing

*Loving God,
be with us and bless us
as we learn ways
that we can follow Jesus
as the first Christians did.
Amen.*

PART 1

 ## What We Already Know

Talk with your children to find out what they already know about the early Church. You can begin the discussion by using the example below or your own words.

There are many stories in the New Testament about the first Christians. What stories about the first Christians do you remember?

 ## What We Will Discover

Provide time for the children to read and complete the activities.

Grade 1 Read pages 77–80 to discover how the first followers of Jesus showed their love for God and for one another.

Grade 2 Read pages 69–72 to discover what we do at Mass today that is similar to what the early Christians did.

Grade 3 Read pages 77–80 to discover what happened to Saul so that he became a follower of Jesus Christ.

Grade 4 Read pages 13–16 to learn about Saint Thomas the Apostle.

Grade 5 Read pages 129–132 to discover what Saint Paul the Apostle wrote to the Christians in 1 Corinthians about the Eucharist.

Grade 6 Read pages 53–56 to discover why the letters in the New Testament were written.

Kindergarten Connection
Faith First Kindergarten Have your child work with another child for this lesson.

Junior High Connection
Faith First Legacy Edition Junior High *Church and Sacraments* Chapter 3, *Morality: Life in Christ* Chapter 4, and *Jesus in the New Testament* Chapter 7

Sharing Together

You can use the following questions to discuss what the children have read. Be sure to answer any questions the children may have. Remember that the responses given below are simply one way to express the main idea underlying the response to each question, so be sure to affirm all appropriate responses.

- *What does it mean to be a Christian?*
  (Christians believe in Jesus and all that he revealed. Christians live as Jesus taught us to live.)

- *How did the first Christians live their faith in Christ?*
  (The first Christians shared all things and cared for people in need. They prayed and listened to the teachings of the Apostles. They broke bread, or took part in the Eucharist, together.)

- *How did the first Christians show their love for one another?*
  (The first Christians shared all things in common. They helped people in need.)

- *What are the names of some of the first Christians?*
  (Responses will vary depending on which grade level textbook the children use.)

- *What are some of the things that Christians do today that are similar to what the first Christians did?*
  (Christians today pray and celebrate the Eucharist. We care for one another. We share our blessings. We learn the teachings of the Apostles.)

All Grades Ask the children to share one or two things that they learned from their reading.

Working Together

Choose one of the following activities to do together or design a similar activity of your own.

- In the early Church the followers of Jesus shared their food with one another. Find out how your family can donate to your parish food pantry or to a local food pantry.

- Find your family's photo albums. Look at the pictures and point out the photos that show people following Jesus and living their faith in Christ by doing things similar to what the first Christians did.

- Each child has learned something about many early Christians who the Church honors as saints. Take the time to see if you can find out more about any of these heroes of our Church.

This week we will . . .

What Difference Does Faith Make?

Provide time for the children to read the "Our Church Makes a Difference" and the "What Difference Does Faith Make in My Life?" pages in their **Faith First Legacy Edition** books and complete the activities on those pages.

Grade 1 Read pages 81 and 82 and ask first graders to share one thing they learned about Saint Martin de Porres and the people who continue his work today. Have the children share their work and their faith choice on page 82.

Grade 2 Read pages 73 and 74 and ask second graders to share two things that they learned about the Bread of Life organization. Have the children share their work and their faith choice on page 74.

Grade 3 Read pages 81 and 82 and ask third graders to share two things that they learned about Saint John Neumann. Have the children share their work and their faith choice on page 82.

Grade 4 Read pages 17 and 18 and ask fourth graders to share two things that they learned about the creeds of the Church. Have the children share their work and their faith decision on page 18.

Grade 5 Read pages 133 and 134 and ask fifth graders to share two things that they learned about letters written by the Church. Have the children share their work and their faith decision on page 134.

Grade 6 Read pages 57 and 58 and ask sixth graders to share two things that they learned about Catholic newspapers. Have the children share their work and their faith decision on page 58.

All Grades Discuss ways family members can help one another keep their faith choice or faith decision.

Kindergarten Connection
Ask the children to share what they learned this week.

Junior High Connection
Ask the children to share two things that they learned about the early Church. Have the children share their faith decisions.

Praying Together

Ask each child to read and share the prayer page for this chapter of the child's book.

Gather your family for prayer.

∞

Light a candle and pray.

Leader: God our Creator,
we are thankful for the time
we have shared today.
Be with us as we pray together.

Reader: (Read aloud Acts of the Apostles 2:42–47.)

∞

Invite each person to say a prayer of petition, asking God to help your family live their faith in Jesus as faithfully as the first Christians; for example, "Lord, help us share with each other."

After each person prays their petition, the rest of the family responds, "Lord, hear our prayer."

∞

Close by joining hands and praying the Our Father aloud. Conclude by sharing a sign of peace.

∞

Be sure to review the "With My Family" page in the child's book. "With My Family" is the last page of each chapter.

The Parables of Jesus

Parables arouse curiosity and attract attention. Parables are stories in which teachers compare one thing that is well known to their readers or listeners to something that is less known. Parables draw listeners to pay attention until they hear how the story comes out. Parables try to persuade listeners to concede a point that they do not perceive as applicable to themselves.

Jesus told parables to teach and to answer questions that he was asked. For example, Jesus taught that the kingdom of God is like a mustard seed (see Luke 13:18–19). By comparing the kingdom of God with a mustard seed, Jesus helped his disciples and other listeners to better understand what the kingdom of God really is. To answer the question "Who is my neighbor?" Jesus told the parable of the Good Samaritan. By comparing the actions of the Samaritan with those of the priest and the Levite, Jesus gave his listeners a much deeper response to the question than his listeners expected.

Using Our Faith First Legacy Edition Books

Use the following chapters to teach this lesson:

Grade 1 · Chapter 6

Grade 2 · Chapter 13

Grade 3 · Chapter 14

Grade 4 · Chapter 9

Grade 5 · Have your fifth grade child share a book with another child for this lesson.

Grade 6 · Chapter 16

Kindergarten Connection
Faith First Kindergarten Chapter 21
Junior High Connection
Faith First Legacy Edition Junior High
Jesus in the New Testament
Chapters 4 and 5

What We Will Learn

Through this lesson your family will learn that:

- One way Jesus teaches us is through stories called parables.
- Parables teach us how to live as children of God.
- Parables teach us about God's love and forgiveness.

Looking for More?

- **www.FaithFirst.com**
- **Faith First Legacy Edition** *Additional Activities* booklet for appropriate age level
- **Faith First** videos (Grade 2— segment 6)
- **Faith First Legacy Edition** *Called to Prayer* booklet for appropriate age level
- Books to read, see pages 16 and 17

Family Blessing

Loving God,
be with us and bless us
as we read about the parables
that Jesus used to teach his disciples.
Help us understand the teachings
of your Son, Jesus Christ.
Amen.

PART 1

What We Already Know

Talk with your children to find out what they already know about the parables of Jesus. You can begin the discussion by using the example below or your own words.

Jesus was a good teacher and a good storyteller. Many of the stories Jesus told are parables. Let's share with one another other some of the parables Jesus told that we remember.

What We Will Discover

Provide time for the children to read and complete the activities.

Grade 1 Read pages 53–56 to discover what the parable of the Good Samaritan teaches us about how we are to treat others.

Grade 2 Read pages 113–116 to discover what the parable about the Forgiving Father tells us about God.

Grade 3 Read pages 121–124 to discover why Jesus told the parable of the Pharisee and the Tax Collector.

Grade 4 Read pages 77–80 to discover why the title Good Shepherd is a good title for Jesus.

Grade 5 Have your child work with another child for this lesson.

Grade 6 Read pages 137–140 to discover the meaning of the parable about the Great Feast.

Kindergarten Connection
Faith First Kindergarten Chapter 21
Junior High Connection
Faith First Legacy Edition Junior High
Jesus in the New Testament Chapters 4 and 5

Sharing Together

You can use the following questions to discuss what the children have read. Be sure to answer any questions the children may have. Remember that the responses given below are simply one way to express the main idea underlying the response to each question, so be sure to affirm all appropriate responses.

■ *What are the two main parts of the Bible?*
(The two main parts of the Bible are the Old Testament and the New Testament.)

■ *What did Jesus teach us in parables?*
(In the parables Jesus taught us how to treat others, how to love God, and how much God loves us. Jesus taught about the kingdom of God.)

■ *Why did Jesus teach in parables?*
(Jesus used his listeners' experience and things they knew about to help them understand the meaning of what he was teaching them.)

All Grades Ask the children to share one or two things that they learned from their reading.

Working Together

Choose one of the following activities to do together or design a similar activity of your own.

■ Choose one of the parables from your children's books and prepare to act it out. You might even want to use simple costumes improvised from things around your home. Act out the parable for children in the neighborhood, for friends, or for relatives.

■ Choose one of the parables from your children's books. Make puppets from brown paper bags and retell the story.

■ Make a book of parables. Illustrate the parables you read in the chapters of your children's books. Make several pictures for each parable. Compile the pictures into a book.

■ Jesus told many parables to teach about the kingdom of God. Read some of these parables and discover what Jesus is teaching: Matthew 13:24–30, 13:31–32, 13:33, 13:44, 13:45–46, 13:47–48, 20:1–16; Mark 4:30–34; and Luke 13:18–19, 13:20–21.

This week we will . . .

What Difference Does Faith Make?

Provide time for the children to read the "Our Church Makes a Difference" and the "What Difference Does Faith Make in My Life?" pages in their **Faith First Legacy Edition** books and complete the activities on those pages.

Grade 1 Read page 57 and 58 and ask first graders to share one thing they learned about the work of Catholic hospitals. Have the children share their work and their faith choice on page 58.

Grade 2 Read pages 117 and 118 and ask second graders to share two things that they learned about Saint John Vianney. Have the children share their work and their faith choice on page 118.

Grade 3 Read pages 125 and 126 and ask third graders to share two things that they learned about Saint Augustine. Have the children share their work and their faith choice on page 126.

Grade 4 Read pages 81 and 82 and ask fourth graders to share two things that they learned about Catholic Relief Services. Ask the children to share their work and their faith decision on page 82.

Grade 5 Have your child work with another child for this lesson.

Grade 6 Read pages 141 and 142 and ask sixth graders to share two things that they learned about the Catholic Campaign for Human Development. Have the children share their work and their faith decision on page 142.

All Grades Discuss ways family members can help one another keep their faith choice or faith decision.

Kindergarten Connection
Ask the children to share what they learned this week.

Junior High Connection
Ask the children to share two things that they learned about parables. Have the children share their faith decisions.

Praying Together

Ask each child to read and share the prayer page for this chapter of the child's book.

Give everyone a minute or two to find an object in your home that symbolizes the parable they read for this lesson. Gather your family for prayer.

∞

Light a candle and pray.

Leader: God our Creator,
we are thankful for the time
we have shared today.
Be with us as we pray together.

Reader: (Read aloud Matthew 13:1–9.)

∞

Ask each person to present their object and pray, "Help us _____." (For example, "be like the Forgiving Father," or "follow the Good Shepherd.") After each person prays their petition, the rest of the family responds, "Amen."

∞

Leader: God our loving Father, help us remember to always follow the example and teachings of your Son, Jesus. Send the Holy Spirit to help us be patient, persistent, and thoughtful when we reflect on your word. We ask this through Christ our Lord.

All: Amen.

∞

Be sure to review the "With My Family" page in the child's book. "With My Family" is the last page of each chapter.

The Teachings of Jesus

In the truest sense of the word, disciples are followers of a teacher. A disciple is also an apprentice, a person who learns by practice from an experienced master teacher. Christians are lifelong disciples and apprentices of the Master Teacher, Jesus Christ. Joined to Jesus Christ through Baptism, we are guided by the Holy Spirit as we learn from Christ to strive for perfection.

Christian discipleship is rooted in the Law of Love taught by Jesus by his word and example. As disciples of Jesus Christ, we are apprentices in living the Law of Love. Disciples of Jesus Christ are challenged with the task of spreading the mission of Jesus by professing our faith in God through both our words and our actions.

Using Our Faith First Legacy Edition Books

Use the following chapters to teach this lesson:

Grade 1 · Chapter 22

Grade 2 · Chapter 19

Grade 3 · Chapter 18

Grade 4 · Chapter 23

Grade 5 · Chapter 19

Grade 6 · Chapter 10

Kindergarten Connection
Faith First Kindergarten Chapter 14
Junior High Connection
Faith First Legacy Edition Junior High
Church and Sacraments Chapter 7 and
Jesus in the New Testament Chapters 3 and 4

What We Will Learn

Through this lesson your family will learn that:

- Jesus teaches us about God's love for us.
- Jesus teaches about the kingdom of God.
- Jesus teaches us to love one another and ourselves.

Looking for More?

- **www.FaithFirst.com**
- **Faith First Legacy Edition** *Additional Activities* booklet for appropriate age level
- **Faith First** videos (Grade 2— segment 3; Grade 4—segment 5; Grade 6—segment 2)
- **Faith First Legacy Edition** *Called to Prayer* booklet for appropriate age level
- Books to read, see pages 16 and 17

Family Blessing

Loving God,
be with us and bless us.
Help us carefully follow
all that your Son, Jesus,
has taught us.
Amen.

PART 1

 What We Already Know

Talk with your children to find out what they already know about the teachings of Jesus. You can begin the discussion by using the example below or your own words.

Jesus teaches us to love God above all else. Jesus also teaches us to love one another. What do these teachings of Jesus mean to you?

 What We Will Discover

Provide time for the children to read and complete the activities.

Grade 1   Read pages 189–192 to discover what Jesus does that shows God's love for all children.

Grade 2   Read pages 165–168 to discover ways we live the Great Commandment.

Grade 3   Read pages 157–160 to discover what Jesus teaches about the Great Commandment.

Grade 4   Read pages 197–200 to discover how the Ten Commandments teach us to live as Jesus taught us.

Grade 5   Read pages 165–168 to discover how each of the Beatitudes helps us understand what it means to be blessed.

Grade 6   Read pages 85–88 to discover what Jesus teaches about how we are to live as his followers.

Kindergarten Connection
Faith First Kindergarten Chapter 14
Junior High Connection
Faith First Legacy Edition Junior High *Church and Sacraments*
Chapter 7 and *Jesus in the New Testament* Chapters 3 and 4

Sharing Together

You can use the following questions to discuss what the children have read. Be sure to answer any questions the children may have. Remember that the responses given below are simply one way to express the main idea underlying the response to each question, so be sure to affirm all appropriate responses.

- *What was the Scripture story about that you read?*
  (Each grade will have a different response, such as Jesus and children, the Great Commandment, the Sermon on the Mount, the Beatitudes, and the kingdom of God.)

- *What does Jesus teach in the Scripture story that you read?*
  (Each grade will have a different response, such as Jesus loves us, God cares for us, live the Great Commandment, live the Beatitudes, do what Jesus did while he was on earth, and so on.)

All Grades Ask the children to share one or two things that they learned from their reading.

Working Together

Choose one of the following activities to do together or design a similar activity of your own.

- Choose one of the Scripture stories that the children have read. Act out that story. Be sure that everyone in your family has a part in the story.

- As a young boy and as an adult, Jesus went to the Temple in Jerusalem. Find out more about the Temple in Jerusalem. You might use your parish or the local library or the Internet as a source for information.

- Make a list of rules that will help your family live as the children of God. Talk about each rule and how it will help you to be fair and loving to others. Post the list of rules on the refrigerator or in another place where family members will see it. Read the list often to remind yourselves how you might live as the children of God.

- Read Matthew 22:34–38. Think up a catchy phrase that encourages people to live the Great Commandment. Write the phrase on poster board, using markers. Display the poster in a place where it can serve as a reminder to the whole family to live the Great Commandment.

This week we will . . .

_____

_____

_____

_____

_____

_____

_____

_____

_____

What Difference Does Faith Make?

Provide time for the children to read the "Our Church Makes a Difference" and the "What Difference Does Faith Make in My Life?" pages in their **Faith First Legacy Edition** books and complete the activities on those pages.

Grade 1 Read page 193 and 194 and ask first graders to share one thing they learned about the Holy Childhood Association. Have the children share their work and their faith choice on page 194.

Grade 2 Read pages 169 and 170 and ask second graders to share two things that they learned about the missionaries of the Church. Have the children share their work and their faith choice on page 170.

Grade 3 Read pages 161 and 162 and ask third graders to share two things that they learned about teaching communities within the Church. Have the children share their work and their faith choice on page 162.

Grade 4 Read pages 201 and 202 and ask fourth graders to share two things that they learned about the Potato Truck Project. Have the children share their work and their faith decision on page 202.

Grade 5 Read pages 169 and 170 and ask fifth graders to share two things that they learned about Habitat for Humanity. Have the children share their work and their faith decision on page 170.

Grade 6 Read pages 89 and 90 and ask sixth graders to share two things that they learned about the Love Truck ministry of one parish. Have the children share their work and their faith decision on page 90.

All Grades Discuss ways family members can help one another keep their faith choice or faith decision.

Kindergarten Connection
Ask the children to share what they learned this week.

Junior High Connection
Ask the children to share two things that they learned about the parables. Have the children share their faith decisions.

Praying Together

Ask each child to read and share the prayer page for this chapter of the child's book.

Give everyone a few minutes to cut out the outline of a paper heart and write on the heart some ways your family can love God and love others. Gather your family for prayer.

Light a candle and pray.

Leader: God our Creator,
we are thankful for the time
we have shared today.
Be with us as we pray together.

Reader: (Read aloud Matthew 22:34–38.)

Ask each person to show their paper heart to the group and say, "Lord, help us to _____." The rest of the family responds, "Help us follow Jesus."

Leader: God our loving Father, help us remember to always follow the example given to us by your Son, Jesus. May we always live the Great Commandment. We ask this through Christ our Lord.

All: Amen.

Be sure to review the "With My Family" page in the child's book. "With My Family" is the last page of each chapter.

The Miracles of Jesus

Most of us have probably had something happen in our lives when we have prayed for a miracle. Or we have heard about something unexpected and unexplainable that has happened, and exclaimed, "It's a miracle!"

In the strict sense of the word, a miracle is "an extraordinary event manifesting divine intervention in human affairs." The Gospel contains stories of the miracles of Jesus. Our immediate response to the miracles of Jesus might be: How could water be changed into wine? How could the sea be calmed? How could a blind man see? These are not the questions of faith. The questions of faith are the "why" questions. Why did Jesus perform miracles? Why did the four Evangelists (Matthew, Mark, Luke, and John) include accounts of the miracles performed by Jesus? These miracle stories in the Gospel help us understand Jesus and the work he came to do. They are signs pointing to the kingdom of God. Jesus' miracles reveal the saving power of God.

Using Our Faith First Legacy Edition Books

Use the following chapters to teach this lesson:

Grade 1 · Chapter 14

Grade 2 · Have your second grade child share a book and work with another child for this lesson.

Grade 3 · Chapter 16

Grade 4 · Chapter 15, see also Chapter 13

Grade 5 · Chapter 4

Grade 6 · Have your sixth grade child share a book and work with another child for this lesson.

Kindergarten Connection
Faith First Kindergarten Have your child work with another child for this lesson.

Junior High Connection
Faith First Legacy Edition Junior High *Mystery of God* Chapter 3, *Church and Sacraments* Chapter 10, and *Jesus in the New Testament* Chapter 3

What We Will Learn

Through this lesson your family will learn that:

- Jesus performed many miracles.
- Miracles are signs of God's love for us.
- Miracles help us know that we can trust God.

Looking for More?

- **www.FaithFirst.com**
- **Faith First Legacy Edition** *Additional Activities* booklet for appropriate age level
- **Faith First** videos (Grade 3—segment 2; Grade 4—segment 2)
- **Faith First Legacy Edition** *Called to Prayer* booklet for appropriate age level
- Books to read, see pages 16 and 17

Family Blessing

*Loving God,
be with us and bless us.
Help us recognize
the miracle of your presence
in each one of us.
Amen.*

PART 1

What We Already Know

Talk with your children to find out what they already know about the miracles of Jesus. You can begin the discussion by using the example below or your own words.

The four Gospels have many stories about Jesus healing people. Let's share with one another one of these stories about Jesus that you remember.

What We Will Discover

Provide time for the children to read and complete the activities.

Grade 1 Read pages 121–124 to discover what Jesus teaches us about God.

Grade 2 Have your child work with another child for this lesson.

Grade 3 Read pages 137–140 to discover what the miracle stories in the Gospels tell us about God.

Grade 4 Read pages 129–132 to discover what the Gospel story about Jesus and Jairus helps us know about God.

Grade 5 Read pages 37–40 to discover why Jesus calmed the sea.

Grade 6 Have your child work with another child for this lesson.

Kindergarten Connection
Faith First Kindergarten Have your child work with another child for this lesson.

Junior High Connection
Faith First Legacy Edition Junior High *Mystery of God* Chapter 3, *Church and Sacraments* Chapter 10, and *Jesus in the New Testament* Chapter 3

Sharing Together

You can use the following questions to discuss what the children have read. Be sure to answer any questions the children may have. Remember that the responses given below are simply one way to express the main idea underlying the response to each question. So, be sure to affirm all appropriate responses.

■ *What miracle story did you read about?*
(Each grade will have a different response, such as Jesus fed a crowd, Jesus turned water into wine, Jesus healed Jairus' daughter, and Jesus calmed the sea.)

■ *What does the miracle story that you read tell us about God?*
(God loves us and cares for us. God is working among us. We are to trust God.)

All Grades   Ask the children to share one or two things that they learned from their reading.

Working Together

Choose one of the following activities to do together or design a similar activity of your own.

■ Talk about some ways your family can show God's love for people, for example, by your family helping and caring for others. Put one of these ideas into action.

■ Read your parish bulletin for examples of the ways your parish community is a sign of God's love for people. How do the actions of the people of your parish show that they are followers of Jesus?

■ Read some of the miracles stories in the Gospel. For example:
• Matthew 8:1–4 (Jesus heals a leper)
• Luke 8:49–56 (Jesus heals Jairus' daughter)
• Luke 5:17–20 (Jesus heals a paralyzed man)
• Luke 18:35–43 (Jesus heals a blind beggar)
• John 2:1–11 (Jesus turns water into wine)

■ Find out whether your parish has a group of people who pray each day for the members in your parish who are sick or who have other special needs. If there is such a group in your parish, contact that group and find out how your family can become part of it.

This week we will . . .

What Difference Does Faith Make?

Provide time for the children to read the "Our Church Makes a Difference" and the "What Difference Does Faith Make in My Life?" pages in their **Faith First Legacy Edition** books and complete the activities on those pages.

Grade 1 Read pages 125 and 126 and ask first graders to share one thing they learned about Operation Rice Bowl. Have the children share their work and their faith choice on page 126.

Grade 2 Have your child work with another child for this lesson.

Grade 3 Read pages 141 and 142 and ask third graders to share two things that they learned about signs of God's love. Have the children share their work and their faith choice on page 142.

Grade 4 Read pages 133 and 134 and ask fourth graders to share two things that they learned about Saint John of God and his followers. Have the children share their work and their faith decision on page 134.

Grade 5 Read pages 41 and 42 and ask fifth graders to share two things that they learned about the work of Catholic Relief Services. Have the children share their work and their faith decision on page 42.

Grade 6 Have your child work with another child for this lesson.

All Grades Discuss ways family members can help one another keep their faith choice or faith decision.

Kindergarten Connection
Ask the children to share what they learned this week.
Junior High Connection
Ask the children to share two things that they learned about miracles of Jesus. Have the children share their faith decisions.

Praying Together

Ask each child to read and share the prayer page for this chapter of the child's book.

Give everyone a few minutes to find or make a symbol of healing and to think of someone who is a caregiver to them. Gather your family for prayer.

Light a candle and pray.
Leader: God our Creator,
we are thankful for the time
we have shared today.
Be with us as we pray together.
Reader: (Read aloud Luke 8:49–56.)

Ask each person to present their symbol and say, "I am thankful for _____ (say the name of a person who is a caregiver)." The other members of the family respond, "*(Name)*, may you trust in God's love for you."

Leader: God, help us remember to always give thanks for the love and care you have for us. May our trust in you grow every day. We ask this through Christ our Lord.

All: Amen.

Be sure to review the "With My Family" page in the child's book. "With My Family" is the last page of each chapter.

Advent

Advent, the first season of the liturgical year, is a time of eager anticipation. During Advent Christians prepare for Christmas, when the Church remembers and celebrates that the Son of God took on flesh and became fully human in all things except sin without giving up his divinity, and lived among us. Advent is also a time of a special kind of eager anticipation. It is a time of hope, a time to celebrate and profess our faith that Christ will come again in glory at the end of time. At the time of Christ's Second Coming, God's loving plan of creation and salvation will finally be realized.

During Advent the Church urges us toward quiet meditation as we make the necessary practical preparations to welcome the Savior at Christmas. We reflect on how we live the mystery and grace of Christ's presence with us. We prepare for the coming of Christ in majesty at the end of time as the Lord and Savior of all creation.

Using Our Faith First Legacy Edition Books

The following pages teach about Advent. We suggest that you focus on the pages listed under "What We Will Discover."

Kindergarten Connection
Faith First Kindergarten Advent/ Christmas, pages 159 and 160
Junior High Connection
Faith First Legacy Edition Junior High
Called to Prayer and Liturgical Seasons
Advent pages

What We Will Learn

Through this lesson your family will learn that:

- Advent helps us prepare for Christmas, the celebration of the coming of Christ among us.
- Advent is a season of joyful expectation and hope.

Looking for More?

- **www.FaithFirst.com**
- **Faith First Legacy Edition** *Additional Activities* booklet for appropriate age level
- **Faith First** videos (Grade 1— segment 6)
- **Faith First Legacy Edition** *Called to Prayer* booklet for appropriate age level
- Books to read, see pages 16 and 17

Family Blessing

Loving God,
be with us and bless us
during this joyful season
as we prepare for the coming
of your Son, Jesus.
Amen.

PART 1

What We Already Know

Talk with your children to find out what they already know about Advent. You can begin the discussion by using the example below or your own words.

During the season of Advent we prepare for the celebration of Christmas. How has our family celebrated Advent in the past?

What We Will Discover

Provide time for the children to read and complete the activities.

Grade 1   Read pages 241–242 to discover for whom we are waiting during Advent.

Grade 2   Read pages 245–246 to discover why Jesus was born in Bethlehem.

Grade 3   Read pages 245–246 to discover how we prepare for Jesus.

Grade 4   Read pages 245–246 to discover what the name *Jesus* means.

Grade 5   Read pages 245–246 to discover how the words and actions of Mary help us celebrate Advent.

Grade 6   Read pages 243–244 to discover how celebrating Advent strengthens our faith in Jesus' presence with us.

Kindergarten Connection
Faith First Kindergarten pages 159 and 160
Junior High Connection
Faith First Legacy Edition Junior High *Called to Prayer and Liturgical Seasons* Advent pages

Sharing Together

You can use the following questions to discuss what the children have read. Be sure to answer any questions the children may have. Remember that the responses given below are simply one way to express the main idea underlying the response to each question, so be sure to affirm all appropriate responses.

- *What do Christians prepare for during Advent?*
  (Christians prepare for the celebration of Christmas. We prepare for the coming of Christ in glory at the end of time.)

- *How do we prepare for Jesus during Advent?*
  (We pray. We help people. We live as lights in the world for others.)

- *What does Mary teach us that can help us celebrate Advent?*
  (Mary teaches us to trust God and to say yes to God.)

All Grades Ask the children to share one or two things that they learned from their reading.

Working Together

Choose one of the following activities to do together or design a similar activity of your own.

- Make an Advent wreath. You can use evergreen branches or just put four candles in a circle on the table. Use three violet candles for the first, second, and fourth weeks of Advent. Use a pink candle for the third week of Advent.

- Make an Advent calendar paper chain. Count the number of days left before Christmas, and make the same number of links to create a paper chain. Each day add a star sticker to a link of the chain. The star sticker represents a kind deed a family member performs that day. On Christmas use the Advent calendar chain as a decoration on your Christmas tree.

- Celebrate the feast of Saint Nicholas on December 6. Read together the story of Saint Nicholas and make simple gifts for one another, such as bookmarks or prayer cards with Scripture verses written on them. Decorate these gifts with the colors of Advent.

- Celebrate the feast of Our Lady of Guadalupe on December 12. Go to the library and find a book telling the story of Blessed Juan Diego and Our Lady. Read the story aloud together.

This week we will . . .

_____

_____

_____

_____

_____

_____

What Difference Does Faith Make?

Provide time for the children to read the pages on Advent in their **Faith First Legacy Edition** books and answer the following questions.

Grade 1 Read page 242 and answer the question, What is one thing you will do to prepare your heart for Jesus?

Grade 2 Read page 246 and answer the question, What is one small thing you will do to show your love for God and for other people?

Grade 3 Read page 242 and answer the question, What is one thing you will do to prepare for Christmas?

Grade 4 Read page 244 and answer the question, What is one thing you will do to prepare the way of the Lord?

Grade 5 Read page 242 and answer the question, What is one thing you will do to help others come to know Jesus?

Grade 6 Read page 242 and answer the question, What is one thing you will do to spread joy during Advent?

All Grades Discuss ways family members can help one another keep their faith choice or faith decision.

Kindergarten Connection
Ask the children to share what they learned this week.
Junior High Connection
Ask the children to share two things they will do during Advent to prepare their hearts to welcome Jesus.

Praying Together

Find a candle that can be safely passed from one person to another. Gather your family for prayer.

Light a candle and pray.

Leader: God our Creator,
we are thankful for the time
we have shared today.
Be with us as we pray together.

Reader: (Read aloud Philippians 4:4–5.)

Pass the candle from one family member to another. As each person holds the candle they say, "Prepare the way of the Lord!" The rest of the family responds, "We are all ready! Come, Lord Jesus, come!"

Leader: God our loving Father, may we who wait for the birth of your Son know the joy of your saving power. May the Holy Spirit help us celebrate the feast of Christmas with love and thanksgiving. We ask this through Christ our Lord.

All: Amen.

Conclude by singing a familiar or favorite Advent hymn together.

Christmas

The liturgical Season of Christmas begins with the celebration of the Vigil of Christmas on Christmas Eve and concludes with the celebration of the feast of the Baptism of the Lord. The season of Christmas is very dear to the hearts of Christians. In the birth of the child Jesus, who is named Savior and Emmanuel, Christ and Lord, we are made new. The whole earth rejoices.

The Christmas season also includes the celebration of the feast of the Holy Family (the Sunday after Christmas or December 30); the Solemnity of Mary, Mother of God (January 1); and Epiphany (the Sunday between January 2 and 8). The feasts celebrated during the Christmas season proclaim to the whole world that Jesus is the Incarnate beloved Son of God, the Savior of the world, on whom God's favor rests.

Delightful traditions of this season manifest the joy of Christians. Gifts are given and received. Evergreens are strung with lights and ornaments. Delicious baked goods are given and received. Special meals are shared. This season of light and generosity reminds us of our vocation as followers of Christ to be lights in the world, to bear gifts, to share our blessings both during this season and throughout the year.

Using Our Faith First Legacy Edition Books

The following pages teach about Christmas. We suggest that you focus on the pages listed under "What We Will Discover."

Grade 1 · Christmas, pages 247–250

Grade 2 · Christmas, pages 247–250

Grade 3 · Christmas, pages 247–250

Grade 4 · Christmas, pages 247–250

Grade 5 · Christmas, pages 247–250

Grade 6 · Christmas, pages 286–289

Kindergarten Connection
Faith First Kindergarten Advent/Christmas, pages 159 and 160; The Holy Family, pages 161 and 162

Junior High Connection
Faith First Legacy Edition Junior High *Called to Prayer and Liturgical Seasons* Christmas pages

What We Will Learn

Through this lesson your family will learn that:

- The angels announced to the shepherds the good news of Jesus' birth.
- The Magi honored Jesus by bringing him gifts.
- Jesus is the Savior of the world and the Prince of Peace.
- The Church honors Mary during the Christmas season.

Looking for More?

- **www.FaithFirst.com**
- **Faith First Legacy Edition** *Additional Activities* booklet for appropriate age level
- **Faith First** videos (Gr. 1—segment 6)
- **Faith First Legacy Edition** *Called to Prayer* booklet for appropriate age level
- Video *Francesco's Friendly World,* "The Gift of Christmas"
- Books to read, see pages 16 and 17

Family Blessing

Loving God,
be with us and bless us
as we celebrate this season
of wonder and awe
when we remember
the birth of Jesus.
Amen.

PART 1

What We Already Know

Talk with your children to find out what they already know about Christmas and the birth of Jesus. You can begin the discussion by using the example below or your own words.

At Christmastime we tell the story of Jesus' birth. Let's share with one another what we remember about this story.

What We Will Discover

Provide time for the children to read and complete the activities.

Grade 1   Read pages 247–248 to discover why the angels visited the shepherds.

Grade 2   Read pages 249–250 to discover how the Magi honored the newborn King, Jesus.

Grade 3   Read pages 249–250 to discover why we call Jesus the Savior of the world.

Grade 4   Read pages 247–248 to discover what the shepherds did when the angels told them about Jesus.

Grade 5   Read pages 247–248 to discover why we say that Jesus is the Prince of Peace.

Grade 6   Read pages 249–250 to discover how the Church honors Mary during the Christmas season.

Kindergarten Connection
Faith First Kindergarten pages 159–162
Junior High Connection
Faith First Legacy Edition Junior High *Called to Prayer and Liturgical Seasons* Christmas pages

Sharing Together

You can use the following questions to discuss what the children have read. Be sure to answer any questions the children may have. Remember that the responses given below are simply one way to express the main idea underlying the response to each question, so be sure to affirm all appropriate responses.

■ *Why did the angels visit the shepherds?*
(The angels told the shepherds about the good news of Jesus' birth.)

■ *How did the Magi honor Jesus?*
(The Magi brought Jesus gifts.)

■ *Why do we call Jesus our Savior?*
(Jesus is the Savior of the world. He is the Promised One, the Savior, God sent to God's people.)

All Grades   Ask the children to share one or two things that they learned from their reading.

Working Together

Choose one of the following activities to do together or design a similar activity of your own.

■ Read together Luke 2:1–20, the Christmas story as told by Luke. After reading the story, ask everyone to share what part of the story they like best.

■ Prepare a short play based on the Christmas story. Use props from around your home or make some simple costumes. Perform the play for relatives and friends whom you visit over the holidays.

■ During the Christmas season we hear the angels proclaim, "Glory to God in the highest!" This is a good time to say or sing the Gloria that is prayed at Mass.

■ Many familiar Christmas carols and hymns tell the story of Jesus' birth. Sing some of your favorite Christmas carols and hymns, for example, "Away in a Manger," "O Little Town of Bethlehem," "Hark! The Herald Angels Sing," "We Three Kings," "Joy to the World," or "Silent Night."

This week we will . . .

What Difference Does Faith Make?

Provide time for the children to read the pages on Christmas in their **Faith First Legacy Edition** books and answer the following questions.

Grade 1 Read page 250 and answer the question, What is one thing you will do to celebrate Christmas?

Grade 2 Read page 250 and answer the question, What is one thing you will say or do to show that you honor Jesus?

Grade 3 Read page 247 and answer the question, What is one thing you will do to rejoice during Christmas?

Grade 4 Read page 248 and answer the question, What is one thing you will do to share the good news of Jesus' birth as the angels did?

Grade 5 Read page 247 and answer the question, What is one thing you will do to show that you are working to build a world of peace?

Grade 6 Read page 247 and answer the question, What is one thing you will do to share the good news of Jesus' birth with others?

All Grades Discuss ways family members can help one another live their faith this Christmas season.

Kindergarten Connection
Ask the children to share what they learned this week.

Junior High Connection
Ask the children to share two things they will do to share with others the good news of Jesus' birth.

Praying Together

Find a candle that you can pass safely from one person to another when it is lighted. Gather your family for prayer.

Light the candle and pray.

Leader: God our Creator,
we are thankful for the time
we have shared today.
Be with us as we pray together.

Reader: (Read aloud Luke 2:8–14.)

Pass the lighted candle from one person to another. As each person holds the candle, the rest of the family says, "Lord, help *(Name)* share the light of Christ with others. Amen."

Leader: God, help us remember to keep the spirit of Christmas alive in our hearts all year long. We ask this through Christ our Lord.

All: Amen.

Conclude by praying the Gloria or singing "Hark! The Herald Angels Sing."

Lent

The days of Lent prepare us to celebrate Easter and welcome new members into the Church. The rites and observances of Lent invite us to strengthen our union with Jesus Christ and to join with him on his journey to Jerusalem, where he was crucified. Throughout Lent the Church constantly proclaims that by dying Jesus brought us new life and taught us how to live as the People of God. Through the cross of Christ new life was given to the whole world.

During Lent we are invited to undertake this journey wholeheartedly through the works of prayer, fasting, and almsgiving. We pray for others and ourselves. We give something up. We share our time and ourselves more generously with other people. These traditional Lenten works remind us that denial and struggle—taking up our cross each day—are essential dimensions of living as disciples of Jesus, ultimately bring new life, and help us prepare for the greatest celebration of the liturgical year, Easter.

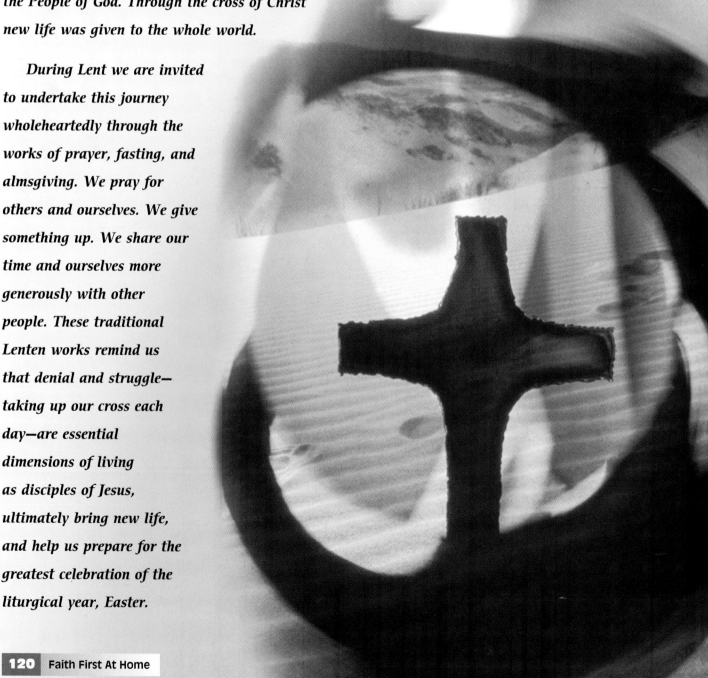

Using Our Faith First Legacy Edition Books

The following pages teach about Lent. We suggest that you focus on the pages listed under "What We Will Discover."

What We Will Learn

Through this lesson your family will learn that:

- Lent helps us prepare for Easter.
- Lent is a time of prayer.
- Lent helps us grow as followers of Jesus.
- Lent helps us grow in our ability to forgive.

Looking for More?

- **www.FaithFirst.com**
- **Faith First Legacy Edition** *Additional Activities* booklet for appropriate age level
- **Faith First** videos (Grade 5—segment 8; Grade 6—segment 8; Junior High *Creed and Prayer*—segment 6; *Liturgy and Morality*—segment 6)
- **Faith First Legacy Edition** *Called to Prayer* booklet for appropriate age level
- Books to read, see pages 16 and 17

Family Blessing

*Loving God,
be with us and bless us
as we reflect on
the journey of Jesus
toward his death
on the cross.
Amen.*

PART 1

 ## What We Already Know

Talk with your children to find out what they already know about Lent. You can begin the discussion by using the example below or your own words.

Each year during Lent Christians do special things to help prepare for celebrating Easter. Let's share with one another some of the things that we remember doing during Lent to prepare for Easter.

 ## What We Will Discover

Provide time for the children to read and complete the activities.

Grade 1   Read pages 255–256 to discover how celebrating Lent helps us grow as followers of Jesus.

Grade 2   Read pages 257–258 to discover how celebrating Lent helps us make more room in our hearts for God.

Grade 3   Read pages 253–254 to discover what it means to be a cheerful giver.

Grade 4   Read pages 259–260 to discover what gift Jesus gave his followers.

Grade 5   Read pages 259–260 to discover why the cross of Christ is central to our celebration of the season of Lent.

Grade 6   Read pages 253–254 to discover God's compassion for people through Jesus.

Kindergarten Connection
Faith First Kindergarten Lent, pages 165 and 166
Junior High Connection
Faith First Legacy Edition Junior High *Called to Prayer and Liturgical Seasons* Lent pages

Sharing Together

You can use the following questions to discuss what the children have read. Be sure to answer any questions the children may have. Remember that the responses given below are simply one way to express the main idea underlying the response to each question, so be sure to affirm all appropriate responses.

■ *How does Lent help us live as followers of Jesus?*
(During Lent we grow closer to Jesus. We pray. We spend time helping others. We think about what Jesus taught. We try to live more like Jesus taught us to live.)

■ *How can we grow in our ability to forgive others as God forgives us?*
(We can recall that God forgives us over and over. We can try our best to treat other people the way Jesus showed us that God treats us. We can participate in the sacrament of Reconciliation.)

■ *What does prayer help us to know and believe?*
(Prayer helps us to know and believe that God is near.)

■ *What do we celebrate on Palm Sunday of the Lord's Passion?*
(We use palm branches and reenact Jesus' entry into Jerusalem. We listen to the story of the Lord's Passion.)

All Grades Ask the children to share one or two things that they learned from their reading.

Working Together

Choose one of the following activities to do together or design a similar activity of your own.

■ During Lent Christians remember Jesus' journey toward his death. Lent is an appropriate time to pray the Stations of the Cross together or plan to take part in your parish's celebration of the Stations of the Cross.

■ Design a plan for using purple to decorate your home environment to remind everyone of the Lenten season. The color purple will remind you to take part in the Lenten practices of praying, fasting, and almsgiving.

■ During Lent Christians take extra time to help other people. Read your parish bulletin to discover the special ways that your parish helps other people during Lent. Plan how your family can participate in one or several of these activities.

■ Lent is a season of preparing for the Easter celebration of new life in Christ. Plant seeds in a container and watch them grow during Lent. Place the container where it will serve as a reminder to the whole family that they too are growing in their life in Christ during Lent.

This week we will . . .

What Difference Does Faith Make?

Provide time for the children to read the pages on Lent in their **Faith First Legacy Edition** books and answer the following questions.

Grade 1 Read page 253 and answer the question, What is one thing you will do to make Lent a special time of prayer?

Grade 2 Read page 258 and answer the question, What is one thing you will do to help someone during Lent this year?

Grade 3 Read page 252 and answer the question, What is one thing you will do to become more like Jesus?

Grade 4 Read page 252 and answer the question, What is one thing you will do to better live the Gospel?

Grade 5 Read page 258 and answer the question, What is one thing you will do to be light for the world?

Grade 6 Read page 251 and answer the question, What is one thing you will do to become more like Jesus?

All Grades Discuss ways family members can help one another live their faith this Lenten season.

Kindergarten Connection
Ask the children to share what they learned this week.
Junior High Connection
Ask the children to share two things that they will do to better live the Gospel and be lights for the world.

Praying Together

Place a candle on a table. Give everyone a minute or two to think about something that they will do this Lenten season and write it on a small piece of paper. Set a basket on the table next to the candle. Gather your family for prayer.

Light the candle and pray.
Leader: God our Creator,
we are thankful for the time
we have shared today.
Be with us as we pray together.
Reader: (Read aloud Matthew 6:1–6.)

Ask each person to place their resolution in the basket while saying, "I will always try my best to live as a follower of Jesus." The rest of the family responds, "*(Name)*, may you know that God is near."

All: *Pray the Lord's Prayer together.*

Leader: God, help us remember to always be generous when it comes to helping or spending time with other people. Prompt us to reach out to people in need with understanding and compassion. We ask this through Christ our Lord.

All: Amen.

Easter

The Easter Triduum is the center of the Church's year. The Easter Triduum is the three-day-long celebration and participation in the great mystery of our faith, the Paschal Mystery of Christ. The celebration of the Easter Triduum begins with the evening celebration of the Lord's Supper on Holy Thursday, continues with the celebration of the Lord's Passion on Good Friday, and concludes with the celebration of Evening Prayer on Easter Sunday.

On Holy Thursday evening we join Christ at the memorial of his final celebration of the Passover meal with his disciples. We learn what it means to serve as Jesus did and we receive Christ's gift of his Body and Blood, the Eucharist. On Good Friday we remember Jesus' great love of us as we celebrate the Lord's Passion and death. On Holy Saturday evening we celebrate the Easter Vigil. We rejoice and proclaim that Jesus is risen and celebrate our new life in Christ. We welcome new members into the Church and renew the promises of our own Baptism.

The celebration of the Solemnity continues on Easter Sunday. The Church continues the celebration of the Resurrection of Jesus for the fifty days of the Easter Season.

Using Our Faith First Legacy Edition Books

The following pages teach about Holy Week and Easter. We suggest that you focus on the pages listed under "What We Will Discover."

Grade 1 · Pages 261–282

Grade 2 · Pages 261–282

Grade 3 · Pages 261–282

Grade 4 · Pages 261–282

Grade 5 · Pages 261–282

Grade 6 · Pages 261–282

Kindergarten Connection
Faith First Kindergarten pages 169 and 170
Junior High Connection
Faith First Legacy Edition Junior High
Called to Prayer and Liturgical Seasons
Triduum and Easter season pages

What We Will Learn

Through this lesson your family will learn that:

- We celebrate Jesus' gift of the Eucharist on Holy Thursday.

- On Good Friday we remember that Jesus suffered and died for us.

- During Easter we celebrate that Jesus was raised from death to new life.

Looking for More?

- **www.FaithFirst.com**
- **Faith First Legacy Edition** *Additional Activities* booklet for appropriate age level
- **Faith First** videos (Gr. 2—segment 7; Gr. 3—segment 6; Gr. 5—segment 8; Gr. 6—segment 8; Junior High *Creed and Prayer*—segment 6; *Liturgy and Morality*—segment 6)
- **Faith First Legacy Edition** *Called to Prayer* booklet for appropriate age level
- Books to read, see pages 16 and 17

Family Blessing

Loving God,
be with us and bless us
as we reflect on
the Paschal Mystery of Christ.
Amen.

PART 1

What We Already Know

Talk with your children to find out what they already know about the Easter Triduum and the Season of Easter. You can begin the discussion by using the example below or your own words.

> *The Easter Triduum and the Easter season are the most important time in the Church's year. What are some of the ways that our family and our parish celebrate these sacred days?*

What We Will Discover

Provide time for the children to read and complete the activities.

Grade 1   Read pages 265–266 to discover what the Church celebrates on Good Friday.

Grade 2   Read pages 267–268 to discover why Easter is the most important season of the Church's year.

Grade 3   Read pages 265–266 to discover why we celebrate Good Friday.

Grade 4   Read pages 267–268 to discover what we celebrate at the Easter Vigil.

Grade 5   Read pages 261–262 to discover how Holy Week helps us grow in forgiveness.

Grade 6   Read pages 267–268 to discover why the Easter season is a time for rejoicing.

Kindergarten Connection
Faith First Kindergarten pages 169 and 170
Junior High Connection
Faith First Legacy Edition Junior High *Called to Prayer and Liturgical Seasons* Triduum and Easter season pages

Sharing Together

You can use the following questions to discuss what the children read. Be sure to answer any questions the children may have. Remember that the responses given below are simply one way to express the main idea underlying the response to each question, so be sure to affirm all appropriate responses.

- *What do we celebrate on Holy Thursday?*
  (We celebrate that Jesus gave us the gift of the Eucharist at the Last Supper. We remember the example of service that Jesus gave us when he washed the disciples' feet.)

- *What do we celebrate on Good Friday?*
  (We remember the Lord's Passion and death. We remember how much Jesus loves us.)

- *What do we celebrate on Easter?*
  (We celebrate that Jesus was raised from death to new life.)

All Grades   Ask the children to share one or two things that they learned from their reading.

Working Together

Choose one of the following activities to do together or design a similar activity of your own.

- On Good Friday Christians recall how much Jesus loves us. He willingly suffered and died for us. Celebrating Good Friday reminds us to share our love with other people. Talk about ways that each of you can share your love with others.

- On Holy Thursday Christians remember that Jesus washed the disciples' feet. Jesus' action reminds us that we too are called to live the new commandment of Jesus and to love one another as he loves us. Read together John 13:1–15 and reenact the Gospel story. Take turns washing each other's feet. You might like to play a recording of instrumental music during the ritual.

- We learn from Jesus that it is important to serve and help one another. Have each person draw and cut out outlines of two paper hands. On one of their paper hands, have each family member write their own name. On the other, have each of them write the name of someone they can help. Post these helping hands where family members can see them until everyone has helped someone.

- Make an Easter banner proclaiming the good news of Easter. On the banner write "Alleluia" or "Jesus is risen" or "This is the day the Lord has made." Decorate the banner and hang it outside your home for all to see.

This week we will . . .

_____

_____

_____

_____

_____

What Difference Does Faith Make?

Provide time for the children to read the Triduum and Easter season pages in their **Faith First Legacy Edition** books and answer these questions.

Grade 1   Read page 266 and answer the question, What is one thing you will do to show your love for Jesus by loving others?

Grade 2   Read page 267 and answer the question, What is one thing you will do to show how important Easter is to you?

Grade 3   Read page 264 and answer the question, What is one thing you will do to serve others as Jesus did?

Grade 4   Read page 269 and answer the question, What is one thing you will do to live as a peacemaker?

Grade 5   Read pages 263 and 264 and answer the question, What is one way you will show your love for others as Jesus asked us to do at the Last Supper?

Grade 6   Read page 272 and answer the question, What is one thing you will do to follow Jesus' command to serve others?

All Grades   Discuss ways family members can help one another live their faith this Easter season.

Kindergarten Connection
Ask the children to share what they learned this week.
Junior High Connection
Ask the children to share two things that they will do to tell others about the good news of Jesus' Resurrection.

Praying Together

Decorate the prayer table with symbols of Easter and our new life in the Risen Christ. Gather your family for prayer.

∾

Light a candle and pray.

Leader: God our Creator,
we are thankful for the time
we have shared today.
Be with us as we pray together.

All: This is the day the Lord has made;
let us rejoice and be glad.

Reader: (Read aloud John 20:1–10.)

∾

All: This is the day the Lord has made;
let us rejoice and be glad.
(*Sing "Alleluia" together.*)

∾

Acknowledgements

Excerpts from "Letters to Families from Pope John Paul II,"
Pope John II, 3rd printing, © 1994, Daughters of St. Paul,
Boston, MA.

Photo Credits

Cover Design: Kristy Howard

Abbreviated as follows: (bkgd) background; (t) top; (b) bottom; (l) left; (r) right; (c) center.

Cover (t), © PictureQuest; cover (c), © Tony Freeman/
Photoeditinc; cover (b), © Walter Hodges/Gettyimages.
Page 3 (t), © Punchstock; 3 (bl), © David Young-Wolff/
Photoeditinc; 3 (br), Myrleen Ferguson Cate/Photoeditinc;
6, © Bill Wittman; 7 (t), Myrleen Ferguson Cate/Photoeditinc;
7 (b), © PictureQuest; 10, © Punchstock; 11, © Thinkstock,
LLC.; 12, © PictureQuest; 18, © Sam Martinez/RCL;
20, © Mark L. Stephenson/Corbis; 24, 28, © Punchstock;
32, © Jim Cummins/Gettyimages; 36, © Roy Morsch/Corbis;
40, © Myrleen Cate/Index Stock; 44, © Bill Wittman; 48,
© Myrleen Ferguson Cate/Photoeditinc; 52, © PictureQuest;
56, © Paul Barton/Corbis; 60, © PictureQuest; 64, © James
Shaffer; 68, © PictureQuest; 72, © Tony Freeman/
Photoeditinc; 76, © PictureQuest; 80, © Nancy Sheehan/
Photoeditinc; 84, © Punchstock; 88, © Myrleen Ferguson
Cate/Photoeditinc; 92, © Thinkstock, LLC.; 96, © Deborah
Davis/Photoeditinc; 100, © PictureQuest; 104, © Walter
Hodges/Corbis; 108, © Phoebe Dunn/PictureQuest; 112,
© The Crosiers/Gene Plaisted, OSC; 116, © Joe Cajero,
Jr./Corbis; 120, 124, © The Crosiers/Gene Plaisted, OSC.